D0108527

Presented to:

_____

Presented by:

_____

Date:

_____

Prayer is a cry of hope.

Anytime Prayers for Everyday People
Copyright © 2006 Bordon-Winters LLC

All rights reserved. No part of this book may be reproduced in any form or by any electronic or mechanical means, including information storage and retrieval systems, without permission in writing from the publisher, except by a reviewer who may quote brief passages in a review.

Project developed by Bordon Books, Tulsa, Oklahoma
Concept: Dave Bordon and Tom Winters
Project Writing: Susan Duke, Bonnie Hanson, Kathryn Deering, Anna Popescu in association with SnapdragonGroup℠ Editorial Services

Warner Faith
Hachette Book Group USA
1271 Avenue of the Americas, New York, NY 10020
Visit our Web site at www.warnerfaith.com

WarnerBooks and the "W" logo are trademarks of Time Inc. or an affiliated company. Used under license by Hachette Book Group USA, which is not affiliated with Time Warner Inc.

Printed in the United States of America
First Edition: November 2006
10 9 8 7 6 5 4 3 2 1

ISBN: 0-446-57934-3

Anytime Prayers
FOR
Everyday People

WARNER
Faith®

New York Boston Nashville

Unless otherwise marked, Scripture quotations are taken from the *Holy Bible: New International Version*®. NIV®. (North American Edition)®. Copyright 1973, 1978, 1984 by International Bible Society. Used by permission of Zondervan Publishing House. All rights reserved.

Scripture quotations marked AMP are taken from *The Amplified Bible, Old Testament*. Copyright © 1965, 1987 by Zondervan Corporation, Grand Rapids, Michigan. *New Testament* copyright © 1958, 1987 by the Lockman Foundation, La Habra, California. Used by permission.

Scripture quotations marked CEV are taken from *The Contemporary English Version*. Copyright © 1995 by the American Bible Society. Used by permission.

Scripture quotations marked KJV are taken from the *King James Version* of the Bible.

Scripture quotations marked MSG are taken from *The Message*. Copyright © by Eugene H. Peterson, 1993, 1994, 1995, 1996. Used by permission of NavPress Publishing Group.

Scripture quotations marked NCV are taken from *The Holy Bible, New Century Version*®. Original work copyright © 1987, 1988, 1991 by Word Publishing. All rights reserved. Used by permission.

Scripture quotations marked NASB are taken from the *New American Standard Bible*®. Copyright © 1960, 1962, 1963, 1968, 1971, 1972, 1973, 1975, 1977, 1995 by The Lockman Foundation. Used by permission.

Scripture quotations marked NLT are taken from *The Holy Bible, New Living Translation*. Copyright © 1996. Used by permission of Tyndale House Publishers, Incorporated, Wheaton, Illinois 60189. All rights reserved.

Scripture quotations marked NRSV are taken from *The New Revised Standard Version Bible*. Copyright © 1989 by the Division of Christian Education of the National Council of the Churches of Christ in the United States of America and are used by permission. All rights reserved.

Scripture quotations marked RSV are taken from the *Revised Standard Version* of the Bible, New Testament section, First Edition, Copyright © 1946, New Testament, Second Edition, Copyright © 1971 by the Division of Christian Education of the Churches of Christ in the United States of America. Used by permission.

Scripture quotations marked TLB are taken from *The Holy Bible, The Living Bible Translation*. Copyright © 1971. Used by permission of Tyndale House Publishers, Incorporated, Wheaton, Illinois 60189. All rights reserved.

Scripture quotations marked NKJV are taken from *The Holy Bible, New King James Version*. Copyright © 1979, 1980, 1982, by Thomas Nelson, Inc. Used by permission.

Contents

Prayers of Praise and Thanksgiving 11
Lifting My Voice to God for Who He Is and What He Has Done for Me

When I want to thank God for His blessings 12

When I want to thank God for His creative genius 14

When I want to thank God for His faithfulness 16

When I want to thank God for His forgiveness 18

When I want to thank God for His generosity 20

When I want to thank God for His goodness 22

When I want to thank God for His grace 24

When I want to thank God for His joy 26

When I want to thank God for His love 28

When I want to thank God for His mercy 30

When I want to thank God for His patience 32

When I want to thank God for His peace 34

When I want to thank God for His presence 36

When I want to thank God for His protection 38

When I want to thank God for His provision 40

When I want to thank God for His salvation 42

When I want to thank God for His wisdom 44

Prayers of Supplication 47
Lifting My Voice to God When I Need Help

When I need to feel God's acceptance 48

When I'm feeling anger 50

When I'm dealing with anxiety 52

When I need a change of attitude 54

When I need help paying my bills 56

When I'm overwhelmed by cares 58

When I'm dealing with change 60

When I'm experiencing confusion 62

When I need courage 64

When I'm struggling with depression 66

When I need to be diligent 68

When I'm dealing with disappointment 70

When I need discernment 72

When I'm feeling discontent 74

When I'm dealing with discouragement 76

When I'm experiencing the pain of divorce 78

When I have doubts 80

When I need endurance 82

When I'm being harassed by my enemies 84

When I've experienced failure 86

When I need faith 88

When I need assurance of God's favor 90

When I'm dealing with fear 92

When I need to forgive 94

When I need help identifying my gifts 96

When I need help pursuing my goals 98

When I need help understanding God's will .100

When I need help understanding God's Word 102

When I'm experiencing grief 104

When I need guidance 106

When I'm searching for happiness 108

When I need physical healing 110

When I need emotional healing 112

When I'm dealing with a sense of helplessness 114

When I need hope 116

When I need a job 118

When I want to know God better 120

When I'm dealing with loneliness 122

When I've suffered a loss 124

When my marriage is in trouble 126

When I'm searching for meaning 128

When I need a miracle 130

When I'm struggling with my past 132

When I need patience 134

When I need peace 136

When I'm suffering persecution 138

When I need protection 140

When I'm feeling sadness 142

When I can't sleep 144
When I need strength 146
When I'm facing temptation 148
When I'm experiencing trials 150
When I need wisdom 152
When I have concerns at work 154

Prayers of Confession 157

Lifting My Voice to God When I Need Forgiveness

When I've made foolish choices 158
When I've become critical and judgmental 160
When I've failed to keep my word 162
When I've been hurtful to others 164
When I've stooped to lies and deception 166
When I've been prideful and arrogant 168
When I've sinned (broken God's laws) 170
When I've neglected my responsibilities 172
When I need to be in right relationship with God 174
When I've exacted vengeance 176

Prayers of Intercession 179

Lifting My Voice to God on Behalf of Others

Prayers for my child:

When my child is struggling with addiction 180
When my child is dealing with conflict 182
When my child is in danger 184
When my child needs discipline 186
When my child needs good friends 188
When my child needs emotional healing 190
When my child needs physical healing 192
When my child is dealing with difficulties at home 194
When my child is not in relationship with God 196
When my child is struggling in school 198

Prayers for my spouse:

When my spouse is struggling with addiction 200
When my spouse is dealing with conflict 202

When my spouse is in danger 204

When my spouse needs guidance 206

When my spouse needs emotional healing 208

When my spouse needs physical healing 210

When my spouse needs a job 212

When my spouse is not in relationship with God 214

When my spouse is unfaithful 216

When my spouse has concerns at work 218

When my spouse needs wisdom 220

Prayers for my friends and family members:

When my friend or family member is struggling with addiction 222

When my friend or family member is dealing with conflict 224

When my friend or family member is in danger 226

When my friend or family member goes through divorce 228

When my friend or family member is struggling with finances 230

When my friend or family member is experiencing grief 232

When my friend or family member needs guidance 234

When my friend or family member needs emotional healing 236

When my friend or family member needs physical healing 238

When my friend or family member has a problem with infertility 240

When my friend or family member is not in relationship with God 242

Prayers for the world around me:

When my church needs to be strengthened 244

When my community needs direction and leadership 246

When my employer needs God's favor 248

When I see injustice in the world around me 250

When my nation needs direction and leadership 252

When I encounter the needy 254

Introduction

God wants to know you—and He wants you to know Him. It's a relationship He has invested His heart in. Does that surprise you? It shouldn't. You are God's most beloved creation, made in His own image. It's natural that He would want to communicate with you, and prayer is the means He has chosen to do just that.

Unfortunately, many people are intimidated by the idea of prayer. God seems so big, so powerful. Why would He care about our puny lives? Why would He want to hear about our troubles or heed our cries for help? The answers to those questions are beyond the scope of our limited understanding, but whatever His reasons, the Bible says He does—care, hear, and answer.

Anytime Prayers for Everyday People contains the prayers of people just like you—people who have ups and downs of every kind. It is our hope that as you pray along with them within the pages of this book, you will feel God's loving touch on your own life.

O Precious Father, as we bow
Before Thy throne today—
We count the many blessings
Thou hast shower'd upon our way.

Author Unknown

Prayers of Praise and Thanksgiving

Lifting My Voice to God
for Who He Is and What He
Has Done for Me

When I want to thank God for His blessings . . .

Praise the LORD, O my soul;
all my inmost being, praise his holy name.
Praise the LORD, O my soul,
and forget not all his benefits.
PSALM 103:1-2

❖

From the fullness of his grace we have all received
one blessing after another.
JOHN 1:16

❖

Blessed be the God and Father of our Lord Jesus Christ,
who has blessed us with every spiritual blessing
in the heavenly places in Christ.
EPHESIANS 1:3 NASB

❖

Every good gift and every perfect gift is from above,
and comes down from the Father of lights, with whom there is
no variation or shadow of turning.
JAMES 1:17 NKJV

. . . I will pray.

Holy Lord,

Lately I've been reflecting on how much You have blessed me, and it brings tears to my eyes as I realize You supply all these things because You love me so much.

I look around my home and see how You have amply provided for all my needs. Comfortable furniture fills my rooms. There is food in the pantry and refrigerator to nourish my body. The clothes in my closet keep me warm in the winter and allow me to be cool in the summer.

I am surrounded by family and friends who love and care about me. Did You place them in my life to help me through the rough patches? It seems that way to me.

I know there are times I don't appreciate You as much as I should. Instead, I grumble and complain about the most insignificant things. That's when You remind me that You are always with me—and that is the biggest and best blessing of all. When I'm happy and joyful, You cheer me up even more. And when I'm feeling low, it helps me to remember that the most precious part of my life is knowing You.

Thank You for being the Giver of bountiful blessings.

Amen.

❖

Reflect upon your present blessings of which
every man has many; not on your past misfortunes of
which all men have some.

Charles Dickens

When I want to thank God for His creative genius . . .

In the beginning God created the heavens and the earth.
GENESIS 1:1 NKJV

❖

He merely spoke, and the heavens were formed,
and all the galaxies of stars.
He made the oceans, pouring them into his vast reservoirs.
Let everyone in all the world—men, women and children
—fear the Lord and stand in awe of him.
PSALM 33:6-8 TLB

❖

You alone are the LORD. You made the heavens, even the
highest heavens, and all their starry host, the earth and all
that is on it, the seas and all that is in them. You give life to
everything, and the multitudes of heaven worship you.
NEHEMIAH 9:6

❖

Look up into the heavens. Who created all the stars?
He brings them out one after another, calling each by
its name. And he counts them to see that none are
lost or have strayed away.
ISAIAH 40:26 NLT

. . . I will pray.

Wonderful Father,

Today as I sat on my patio watching the sun rise, I couldn't help it—I lost myself in Your exquisite heavenly canvas of brilliant reds, gleaming oranges, and sun-drenched yellows. How breathtaking it is to gaze at this marvelous gift that You created for us to enjoy!

Thank You for this brand-new day and the chance it gives me to consider how amazing and awesome You are to have formed everything just by thinking it into existence. How can I witness this and not believe that You created all of it?

What a treat it is to visit this magnificent open-air art gallery without having to leave home. A soft mist drapes itself over everything, casting the distant majestic mountains and nearby rolling hills into early morning purple hues. Your artistic touch is evident in the exquisite flowers and plants that open themselves up to Your sunshine and drink in the refreshing droplets of the morning dew.

Help me to always hold on to the joy and hope I have right now in knowing You made all of this for my enjoyment. You are an amazing God.

Amen.

❋

Creativity is the basic attribute of God,
identical with His uniqueness.

Hermann Cohen

When I want to thank God for His faithfulness . . .

Even when we are too weak to have any faith left,
[Christ] remains faithful to us and will help us,
for he cannot disown us who are part of himself,
and he will always carry out his promises to us.
2 TIMOTHY 2:13 TLB

❖

I face your Temple as I worship, giving thanks to you for all
your lovingkindness and your faithfulness, for your promises
are backed by all the honor of your name.
PSALM 138:2 TLB

❖

All the paths of the LORD are steadfast love and faithfulness,
for those who keep his covenant and his testimonies.
PSALM 25:10 RSV

❖

Your love, O LORD, reaches to the heavens,
your faithfulness to the skies.
PSALM 36:5

. . . I will pray.

Most Trustworthy Father,

I used to think I could depend on others to help me through the tough times, but lately You've shown me that the only one I can trust in is You. Any time I'm feeling lonely, frustrated, discouraged, weak, or tired, I can count on You for comfort and encouragement.

More than anyone else, You know and understand my struggles, and You're always here to encourage me. I look to You now, Lord, for what only You can give me during this time of trial.

Sometimes I feel so overwhelmed that all I can do is close my eyes and whisper Your name. I imagine Your arms surrounding me like a warm blanket, soothing me, keeping me safe. No one else is here—but You. You're always here, loving me through all the days of my life.

And, Lord, I commit my family and friends to Your faithful care as well. I know they love me, but they're only human. They fail me at times, just as I fail them. You are the only constant in our world. You are everlastingly faithful.

Amen.

❊

God's investment in us is so great
He could not possibly abandon us.

Erwin W. Lutzer

When I want to thank God for His forgiveness . . .

If we confess our sins, He is faithful and just to forgive us our sins and to cleanse us from all unrighteousness.

1 JOHN 1:9 NKJV

❖

*If You, LORD, should mark iniquities,
O Lord, who could stand?
But there is forgiveness with You.*

PSALM 130:3-4 NASB

❖

*You are forgiving and good, O Lord,
abounding in love to all who call to you.*

PSALM 86:5

❖

*All the prophets testify about him that everyone who believes
in him receives forgiveness of sins through his name.*

ACTS 10:43

. . . I will pray.

Benevolent Father,

It happened again. Just when I started feeling as if things were going well, I messed up. Instead of keeping my focus on You, I let myself be pulled into a bad situation—something that is not what You want for me and certainly does not glorify You. How does this keep happening? Never mind, I know. You try to warn me, but I always insist on going my own way.

Forgive me, Lord—again. Wash me clean and help me to be vigilant, listening carefully to Your Spirit inside my heart. My desire is to please You, but we both know that I can't make that a reality without Your help. Let me live ever aware of Your presence. As I practice living in Your presence, I believe that sin will lose its power over me.

I know, Lord, that You are a kind, loving, and merciful God, and I know You desire only the best for me. I am so thankful for Your willingness to forgive me each and every time. I praise You above all others, for You are the one who has washed me clean.

Amen.

❉

When God pardons, He consigns the offense
to everlasting forgetfulness.

Merv Rosell

When I want to thank God for His generosity . . .

To him who is able to do immeasurably more than all we ask or imagine, according to his power that is at work within us, to him be glory in the church.

EPHESIANS 3:20-21

❈

Generous to a fault,
you [God] lavish your favor on all creatures.

PSALM 145:16 MSG

❈

All sunshine and sovereign is GOD,
generous in gifts and glory.
He doesn't scrimp with his traveling companions.

PSALM 84:11 MSG

❈

Splendor and beauty mark his craft;
His generosity never gives out.
His miracles are his memorial.

PSALM 111:3-4 MSG

. . . I will pray.

Bountiful God,

How can I look at my life and not be thankful for everything You have given me? I'm not referring to material possessions, although I am grateful for all those blessings. I'm thinking of the magnificent ways You help me get through each day.

When I need patience, I reach out to You—and You're there. When I need courage—I reach out and You're there. When I need hope, joy, faith—You're there. You're always there with all I need to face each day with dignity.

Some people would say that You are generous to a fault! I know You don't have any faults, Lord, but it's partly true. You give me so much more than I could ever even imagine, far more than I could ever ask for.

Thank You, Lord, for opening Your generous arms and bestowing on me so many blessings. Thanks for meeting my every need. Show me ways to be generous with others in return. I want to be like You in every way, but especially in this way— I want to be called "generous to a fault" in honor of my heavenly Father.

Amen.

❊

Accustom yourself to the wonderful thought
that God loves you with a tenderness, a generosity,
and an intimacy that surpasses all your dreams.

Abbe Henri de Tourville

When I want to thank God for His goodness . . .

The LORD is good to all,
And His mercies are over all His works.

PSALM 145:9 NASB

✤

I am still confident of this:
I will see the goodness of the LORD
in the land of the living.

PSALM 27:13

✤

How great is your goodness,
which you have stored up for those who fear you,
which you bestow in the sight of men
on those who take refuge in you.

PSALM 31:19

✤

In his goodness he chose to make us his own children by
giving us his true word. And we, out of all creation, became
his choice possession.

JAMES 1:18 NLT

. . . I will pray.

Loving Father,

I used to think of myself as a good person. I felt great about that, but now I know that the goodness in my soul is little more than a faint reflection of the goodness I see in You every day. You are good in every way—without exception. I am good only as I keep my heart tuned in and submitted to You.

That's easy to say, but not always so easy to do. I mean to be listening every minute, letting You oversee my motives, my actions, my words. But somehow the not-so-good part of me keeps getting through.

Lord, I know that I'll never be as good as You are—not in this life. But I know that You, Lord, can help me to be a much better person than I am right now. Work with me. Keep me on my toes. Let Your goodness flow through me to everyone I know.

You are so excellent, Lord. It's an honor to be Your child, an honor to be able to learn from You and draw from Your utter perfection. Thank You, Lord, for Your goodness.

Amen.

❁

The Lord's goodness surrounds us at every moment.
I walk through it almost with difficulty,
as through thick grass and flowers.

R. W. Barbour

When I want to thank God for His grace . . .

From his fullness we have all received, grace upon grace.
The law indeed was given through Moses;
grace and truth came through Jesus Christ.
JOHN 1:16-17 NRSV

❖

Even though on the outside it often looks like things are falling
apart on us, on the inside, where God is making new life,
not a day goes by without his unfolding grace.
2 CORINTHIANS 4:16 MSG

❖

The amazing grace of the Master, Jesus Christ,
the extravagant love of God, the intimate friendship of
the Holy Spirit, be with all of you.
2 CORINTHIANS 13:14 MSG

❖

If your life honors the name of Jesus, he will honor you.
Grace is behind and through all of this, our God giving
himself freely, the Master, Jesus Christ, giving himself freely.
2 THESSALONIANS 1:12 MSG

. . . I will pray.

Most Compassionate God,

Where would I be without Your grace—full and free and wonderful? It picks up in the very spot where I leave off, tucker out, and finishes the job for me. When I'm too frail to do the right thing, Your grace gives me the boost I need to finish in the winner's circle. When I find it impossible to forgive, to believe, to go on, Your grace shows me a way where there is no way. Your grace is more than amazing—it's astonishing!

Lord, I want to thank You for Your grace. I heard somewhere that it stands for **G**od's **R**iches **A**t **C**hrist's **E**xpense. I'll never understand it, giving me so much when I'm so completely undeserving. I guess it's pretty hard to explain.

Help me, Father, to find ways to pass along the message of Your grace to my friends and family. Some of them don't know how much You love them. They've never experienced Your grace—even though it has always been there, poured out for them just as it was for me. Don't let me miss even one opportunity, Lord, to pass on to others Your riches, purchased by Your precious Son.

Amen.

❄

Grace comes into the soul,
as the morning sun into the world;
first a dawning, then a light;
and at last the sun in his full and excellent brightness.

Thomas Adams

When I want to thank God for His joy . . .

Shout for joy to the LORD, all the earth.
Worship the LORD with gladness;
come before him with joyful songs.
PSALM 100:1-2

❖

[The Lord says] The joy of the LORD will fill you to
overflowing. You will glory in the Holy One of Israel.
ISAIAH 41:16 NLT

❖

We are praying . . . that you will be filled with his mighty,
glorious strength so that you can keep going no matter
what happens—always full of the joy of the Lord.
COLOSSIANS 1:11 TLB

❖

You will make known to me the path of life;
In Your presence is fullness of joy.
PSALM 16:11 NASB

❖

Be full of joy in the Lord always.
I will say again, be full of joy.
PHILIPPIANS 4:4 NCV

. . . I will pray.

Glorious Father,

Today I woke up singing a praise song that I heard on the radio yesterday. I guess it must have settled into my mind because I remember hearing it play through my dreams during the night as I slept. What a wonderful way to start the day! No matter how tired, cranky, or achy I feel when I wake up, praising You in song overcomes any pain or irritation I may be experiencing.

There are so many reasons to be joyful when thinking about You. Knowing I can always turn to You for guidance makes me smile with gratification. Your comforting arms holding me close make me sigh in blissful contentment.

Your heavenly joy becomes visible when I hear the delighted giggling of a child or see the tiny hands and feet of a newborn baby. And how can I not rejoice with You when a glorious rainbow paints the sky? I always appreciate Your readiness to show me the joys in life, especially when I'm at my lowest. You give me joy enough for each and every day. Thank You for Your gracious gift.

Amen.

❖

I have no understanding of a long-faced Christian.
If God is anything, He must be joy.

Joe E. Brown

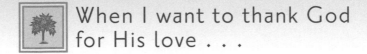

When I want to thank God for His love . . .

God's love will continue forever.
PSALM 52:1 NCV

❖

This is what real love is: It is not our love for God;
it is God's love for us in sending his Son to be
the way to take away our sins.
1 JOHN 4:10 NCV

❖

Give thanks to the LORD, for he is good;
his love endures forever.
PSALM 118:29

❖

[Jesus said] God so loved the world that he gave
his one and only Son, that whoever believes in him
shall not perish but have eternal life.
JOHN 3:16

❖

We love Him because He first loved us.
1 JOHN 4:19 NKJV

. . . I will pray.

Loving Father,

I don't get it, Lord—why You love me, that is. I look myself over, and frankly, I must not be seeing what You see. I can't understand it. But I've decided that I don't need to understand it. Why, even the nature and logic of love between human beings is seldom knowable. That's why I've determined just to accept it, to let Your love cover me, change me, energize me, make me special.

I've read in the Bible that You love me so much that You allowed Your Son, Jesus Christ, to accept the punishment for my sins. I can't imagine giving up one of my children for anyone—even You. I guess that's why You're God and I'm just a mortal human being created in Your image and loved for Your own reasons.

Thank You, Father, for Your great love for me . . . and I want You to know that Your love won't be scorned. I love You in return. With all of my human strength, I love You. With all of my human determination, I pledge my love to You. I don't deserve Your love, Father, but You do deserve mine. I give it freely.

Amen.

❋

God does not love us because we are valuable.
We are valuable because God loves us.

Archbishop Fulton J. Sheen

When I want to thank God for His mercy . . .

All those who know your mercy, Lord, will count on you for help. For you have never yet forsaken those who trust in you.
PSALM 9:10 TLB

❖

I will always trust in you and in your mercy and shall rejoice in your salvation. I will sing to the Lord because he has blessed me so richly.
PSALM 13:5-6 TLB

❖

Generous in love—God, give grace! Huge in mercy—wipe out my bad record.
PSALM 51:1 MSG

❖

God is sheer mercy and grace; not easily angered, he's rich in love.
PSALM 103:8 MSG

❖

You can't whitewash your sins and get by with it; you find mercy by admitting and leaving them.
PROVERBS 28:13 MSG

. . . I will pray.

Gracious Lord,

I read in the Bible today about the blind man who called out, "Lord, have mercy on me." I'm not blind, but I sure do know what it's like to need mercy—Your mercy. It seems as if I mess up constantly. You know how hard I try, Lord, but it seems as if I'm always doing those things that I try not to do. My thoughts wander, my temper flares, my priorities get rear-ended. Bam! I'm back on the side of the road begging for Your mercy again.

What amazes me is that every time I cry out to You, You hear me. I pour out my sin to You and there You are, forgiving, loving, encouraging me to stand up, brush myself off, and get back to living my life.

I want You to know how grateful I am for Your mercy. I've read a little about the gods of other religions—stone gods, unable to speak, unable to love, unable to offer mercy. My heart is gladdened to the point of tears, Lord, as I consider my God, my loving, merciful, caring God. Thank You from the bottom of my heart.

Amen.

❈

Our faults are like a grain of sand beside the great mountain of the mercies of God.

Saint Jean Baptiste Marie Vianney

When I want to thank God for His patience . . .

The Lord is not slow about His promise,
as some count slowness, but is patient toward you, not
wishing for any to perish but for all to come to repentance.
2 PETER 3:9 NASB

❧

God had mercy on me, so that Christ Jesus could
use me as a prime example of his great patience with
even the worst sinners.
1 TIMOTHY 1:16 NLT

❧

The fruit of the Spirit is . . . patience.
GALATIANS 5:22 NASB

❧

With patience you can convince a ruler,
and a gentle word can get through to the hard-headed.
PROVERBS 25:15 NCV

❧

The patient in spirit is better than the proud in spirit.
ECCLESIASTES 7:8 RSV

. . . I will pray.

Father God,

How do You do it? How do You keep from losing it with me the tenth, twentieth, one thousandth time I blow it and go against You? I have to tell You, I would be through after the third or—in a frenzy of amazing patience—the fourth time someone has done me wrong. Yet You stand by me, keep on loving me, forgive me over and over again. It seems crazy, but I suppose it's divine.

Forgive me when I push Your patience to the outer limits. I submit myself to You once again. I want to be pleasing to You, to be obedient to Your will. I do—really. Not that You would know that by my actions. Search my heart, Lord. It is Yours. Look closely and You'll see Your mark there.

I'm grateful for Your wonderful patience, Lord. But I know that even You have limits. Show me how to listen more carefully to Your voice, to obey You quickly without reservation and without hesitation. And help me to practice patience in my own life, offering to others what You have freely given me.

Amen.

❊

God's love for poor sinners is very wonderful,
but God's patience with ill-natured saints is
a deeper mystery.

Henry Drummond

When I want to thank God for His peace . . .

The punishment that brought us peace was upon him.
ISAIAH 53:5

❖

[Jesus said] I am leaving you with a gift
—peace of mind and heart!
And the peace I give isn't fragile like
the peace the world gives.
So don't be troubled or afraid.
JOHN 14:27 TLB

❖

Following after the Holy Spirit leads to life and peace.
ROMANS 8:6 TLB

❖

Let the peace of heart which comes from Christ be always
present in your hearts and lives, for this is your responsibility
and privilege as members of his body.
COLOSSIANS 3:15 TLB

❖

While they were still talking about this, Jesus himself stood
among them and said to them, "Peace be with you."
LUKE 24:36

. . . I will pray.

Kindest Lord,

Thanks so much for Your peace. I feel it pouring over me right now, absorbing my problems, clearing my mind, opening my heart to hear Your voice. I don't know why I didn't come to You sooner—too caught up in all the confusion, I guess.

It's been quite a day—actually quite a week. So much has been going on. So many loose ends. I was feeling like an old, frayed shag rug until You came on the scene and settled me down. Now I feel as placid as a deep, glassy mountain lake.

Lord, I want You to know that I don't take this peace for granted. I know that it comes from knowing You are in control of my life. When I come to You and give You my concerns, You take them and then say, "I've taken care of everything. Stay—rest a moment in My presence."

I know that this peace I'm feeling was bought at a staggering price, and yet, it's free to me for the asking. Thank You for letting me take it with me as I leave this sacred place and step back into the world.

Amen.

✤

God is a tranquil being and abides in a tranquil eternity. So must Your spirit become a tranquil and clear little pool, wherein the serene light of God can be mirrored.

Gerhard Tersteegen

When I want to thank God for His presence . . .

*God has made you his friends again. He did this through
Christ's death in the body so that he might bring you into
God's presence as people who are holy.*

COLOSSIANS 1:22 NCV

❖

*Be still in the presence of the LORD,
and wait patiently for him to act.*

PSALM 37:7 NLT

❖

*Wonderful times of refreshment will come from
the presence of the Lord.*

ACTS 3:20 NLT

❖

*I was filled with delight day after day,
rejoicing always in his presence.*

PROVERBS 8:30

❖

Let us come before His presence with thanksgiving.

PSALM 95:2 NKJV

. . . I will pray.

Precious Father,

Tonight is something special. I can really feel Your presence as I kneel here by my bed. I even caught myself looking over just now, searching for You with my eyes. That's how aware I am that You're right here in the room with me. I hope it will always be this way.

But I've learned that sometimes I can't feel Your presence at all. I can't count on my feelings—but I can count on other things, for example, such as Your Word. My Bible says You are always with me, whether I feel You or not. I believe that. Other times, I feel You near me—not because of my feelings but because I see what You are doing—circumstances changing, people bending, miracles happening. At those times, I know You are watching and moving on my behalf.

Still, nothing compares to these extraordinary times when Your presence seems to be so tangible, as close as my breath. At times like this, I feel completely safe, as if nothing can touch me—no problem, no trial, no negative thought or emotion. Thank You, Lord, for Your presence in, around, and through my life.

Amen.

＊

As His child, you are entitled to His kingdom,
The warmth, the peace, and the power
of His presence.

Author Unknown

When I want to thank God for His protection . . .

The LORD loves the just and will not forsake his faithful ones.
They will be protected forever.
PSALM 37:28

❊

Happy are those who trust him for protection.
PSALM 2:12 NCV

❊

Let all who take refuge in you be glad;
let them ever sing for joy.
Spread your protection over them,
that those who love your name
may rejoice in you.
PSALM 5:11

❊

He shall give His angels charge over you,
To keep you in all your ways.
PSALM 91:11 NKJV

. . . I will pray.

O God,

This is one scary world. There are wars, floods, earthquakes, hurricanes, tornadoes, terrorists, criminals, sickness, injury, and way too many harms for me even to name. Sometimes it's just overwhelming—thinking about tragedies, both large and small, and realizing that I can do nothing much at all to protect myself and those I love.

When I feel the panic rising, though, that's when I pause and think about You. No matter what, I know You won't be caught off guard. You always know what's coming, and You are always there to help me through every trial and hardship. Just knowing You're there for me, that Your mighty hand is protecting me—that means more than any insurance policy.

After all, You protected Noah and his family in that megaflood. You kept Daniel safe in the lions' den. I know You will help me when I need it as well. You know, Lord, I do understand that I live here in this imperfect world, where stuff happens. . . . But I also know that You will never desert me. In the midst of my gravest trial or calamity, You will be right there with me—loving me, strengthening me, and guarding me.

Amen.

❖

In the morning prayer is the key that opens to us
the treasures of God's mercies and blessings;
in the evening, it is the key that shuts us up under His
protection and safeguard.

Jacques Ellul

When I want to thank God for His provision . . .

My God shall supply all your need according to
his riches in glory by Christ Jesus.
PHILIPPIANS 4:19 KJV

❖

[Jesus said] Don't worry about food—what to eat and drink;
don't worry at all that God will provide it for you.
All mankind scratches for its daily bread, but your
heavenly Father knows your needs. He will always
give you all you need from day to day if you will
make the Kingdom of God your primary concern.
LUKE 12:29-31 TLB

❖

He provides food for those who fear him;
he is ever mindful of his covenant.
PSALM 111:5 RSV

❖

His divine power has given us everything needed for life and
godliness, through the knowledge of him who called us
by his own glory and goodness.
2 PETER 1:3 NRSV

. . . I will pray.

Gracious Father,

I'm getting ready for a camping trip and realize I don't have everything I need. My tent and sleeping bag will give me protection at night. I'll take my poncho in case it rains and some warm clothing in preparation for the predicted cold weather. My list includes enough food and beverages for the weekend, various cooking implements, a flashlight and lantern to enable me to see after dark, and various medications I need to take. I check off each of these items against my list, but it seems that I'm forgetting something, some provision. What could it be?

We both know that I know what's missing, Lord. I can cover the easy stuff—food, beverages, pans—but I need Your help to see to the things I can't: the unseen, the unexpected, the unplanned.

Thank You for all You supply on my behalf. You're like a hedge of protection around me, providing me with whatever I need to face a weekend campout or an everyday circumstance. Thank You, my Lord. I wouldn't think of going anywhere without You.

Amen.

❖

God is absolutely unlimited in His ability and
His resources. And He is unlimited in His desire to
pour out those resources upon us.

Gloria Copeland

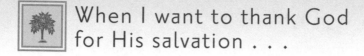

When I want to thank God for His salvation . . .

I am not ashamed of the gospel: it is the power of God
for salvation to every one who has faith.
ROMANS 1:16 RSV

�֎

I tell you, now is the time of God's favor,
now is the day of salvation.
2 CORINTHIANS 6:2

✷

The LORD lives, and blessed be my rock;
And exalted be the God of my salvation.
PSALM 18:46 NASB

✷

[Peter said] Jesus is the only One who can save people.
His name is the only power in the world that has been given
to save people. We must be saved through him.
ACTS 4:12 NCV

✷

If you confess with your mouth the Lord Jesus and
believe in your heart that God has raised Him from the dead,
you will be saved.
ROMANS 10:9 NKJV

. . . I will pray.

Redeeming Lord,

I am always amazed when I consider the depth of Your love for me. You, who created everything in the universe, care for me so much You sent Your Son, Jesus Christ, to die for my sins. And I will never be able to explain why Jesus came—willingly, determined to rescue me and make me part of Your family. My salvation is more wonderful and amazing than I could ever comprehend.

Lord, You could have simply walked away from Your human creation, washed Your hands, and moved on to a new project. Instead, You walked beyond Your personal disappointment and went to extraordinary, even miraculous, lengths to salvage us. Knowing that moves me beyond words. And then to think that even in the face of so great a gesture toward us, You've made Yourself vulnerable by leaving us with the choice to take Your gift or leave it.

I want to be very clear, Lord—I take it! Every bit of it—all You have or want or plan for me! I choose to love You back every day of my life. Thank You for Your lavish gift of salvation.

Amen.

It is not your hold of Christ that saves you,
but His hold of you!

Charles Haddon Spurgeon

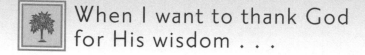

When I want to thank God for His wisdom . . .

God's wisdom is deep, and his power is great.
JOB 9:4 NCV

❖

Wisdom will make your life pleasant and will bring you peace. As a tree produces fruit, wisdom gives life to those who use it, and everyone who uses it will be happy.
PROVERBS 3:17-18 NCV

❖

God's words will always prove true and right, no matter who questions them.
ROMANS 3:4 TLB

❖

O LORD, how manifold are your works! In wisdom you have made them all; the earth is full of your creatures.
PSALM 104:24 NRSV

❖

Though he brings grief, he also shows compassion according to the greatness of his unfailing love. For he does not enjoy hurting people or causing them sorrow.
LAMENTATIONS 3:32-33 NLT

. . . I will pray.

Heavenly Father,

So many questions are bumping around in this head of mine. Questions without answers—at least for now. Why are so many lives destroyed by disease and natural disasters, for example? Why are some babies born with serious disabilities that will mean difficult—and possibly shortened—lives for them? Why do some ungodly people accumulate great wealth while many of the most humble and loving people I know struggle with their finances? I have asked these questions of other people, but they haven't been much help. The answer is always, "Only God in His great wisdom knows." So . . . that's why I'm here, Lord. I've come straight to the source.

Maybe You'll answer my questions now and maybe I'll have to wait until I get to heaven to find out. Maybe I'll never find out at all, but this much I am sure of: As inexplicable as these things might seem to me, I know that You are just and good and will turn all those things in my life that were meant for evil into good. After all, You aren't just wise, You're wisdom personified. I trust You, Lord, and I submit to Your wisdom concerning these matters—whether I ever understand the "whys" or not. Even when I don't have the answers, I trust that You do.

Amen.

❋

Most of us go through life praying a little, planning a little,
. . . hoping but never being quite certain of anything,
and always secretly afraid that we will miss the way. . . .
There is a better way. It is to repudiate our own wisdom
and take instead the infinite wisdom of God.

A. W. Tozer

Were half the breath that's vainly spent,
To heaven in supplication sent,
Our cheerful song would oftener be,
"Hear what the Lord has done for me."

Garnet Rolling

Prayers of Supplication

Lifting My Voice to God
When I Need Help

When I need to feel God's acceptance . . .

The God and Father of our Lord Jesus Christ . . .
made us accepted in the Beloved.
EPHESIANS 1:3,6 NKJV

✤

[Jesus said] The one who comes to Me
I will certainly not cast out.
JOHN 6:37 NASB

✤

Christ accepted you, so you should accept each other,
which will bring glory to God.
ROMANS 15:7 NCV

✤

"Return to me," declares the LORD Almighty, "and I will
return to you," says the Lord Almighty.
ZECHARIAH 1:3

✤

Peter began to speak: "I now realize how true it is that
God does not show favoritism but accepts men from every
nation who fear him and do what is right."
ACTS 10:34-35

. . . I will pray.

Heavenly Father,

It's tough out there. Troubles seem to follow me everywhere I go. No matter how hard I try, someone always seems to be letting me know I've failed—my boss, my kids, even my spouse. Maybe I have—I just don't know anymore. What I do know is that I need to spend some time here with You, regaining my perspective, renewing my courage, and soaking up Your unconditional acceptance.

I love knowing that even when I mess up, You continue to love me. Not only that, but You see my heart and recognize my motives. That's such a relief, especially when everyone around me is questioning every decision I make and every step I take.

Lord, help me to pass on Your pure and constant acceptance to others as well. If I'm feeling this way, I'm sure a lot of other people in my life are too. Some of them may need to feel Your acceptance even more than I do now.

And, Father, for those times when I have to do the difficult thing that no one understands or agrees with, help me to remember that Your acceptance is enough—more than I will ever need.

Amen.

❉

Accept that fact that you are accepted.

Paul Tillich

When I'm feeling anger . . .

Patience is better than strength.
Controlling your temper is better than capturing a city.
PROVERBS 16:32 NCV

❖

Put them all aside: anger, wrath, malice, slander,
and abusive speech from your mouth.
COLOSSIANS 3:8 NASB

❖

Refrain from anger and turn from wrath;
do not fret—it leads only to evil.
PSALM 37:8

❖

Do not be quickly provoked in your spirit,
for anger resides in the lap of fools.
ECCLESIASTES 7:9

❖

You must understand this, my beloved:
let everyone be quick to listen, slow to speak, slow to anger;
for your anger does not produce God's righteousness.
JAMES 1:19-20 NRSV

. . . I will pray.

Righteous Father,

You know how I struggle to control my anger sometimes. Usually I'm pretty even tempered, but every once in a while I get pushed too far and then boom, I totally blow it. At times like that, I wonder, *Who is that horrible person and how did she get inside me?*

Lord, I don't want any area of my life to be out of control. I want all of my life to be pleasing to You. Unfortunately, I just can't seem to make it happen—not by myself anyway.

I need Your help. Show me when I'm getting to the breaking point. Give me a nudge so that I recognize what is about to happen before it's too late. Then, Lord, show me how to free myself from the situation. The Bible says that You will make a way of escape for us when we are tempted, and that's exactly what I'm asking You to do.

I realize that an escape route works only if I'm willing to take it. And, well . . . that's what I can do for You—promise that if You show me, I'll take Your gracious way out. Thank You for helping me keep anger at a distance in my life.

Amen.

❈

When angry, take a lesson from technology;
always count down before blasting off.

Author Unknown

When I'm dealing with anxiety . . .

When anxiety was great within me,
your consolation brought joy to my soul.
PSALM 94:19

❖

Cast all your anxiety on him because he cares for you.
1 PETER 5:7

❖

Anxiety weighs down the human heart,
but a good word cheers it up.
PROVERBS 12:25 NRSV

❖

Be anxious for nothing, but in everything by prayer and
supplication, with thanksgiving, let your requests be made
known to God; and the peace of God, which surpasses all
understanding, will guard your hearts and minds through
Christ Jesus.
PHILIPPIANS 4:6-7 NKJV

❖

May God bless you richly and grant you increasing freedom
from all anxiety and fear.
1 PETER 1:2 TLB

. . . I will pray.

Loving Father,

Edgy, anxious, jumpy—I just can't seem to get it together this morning. Every little detail seems to be a big deal doing its dance across my mind. I really need Your help, Your peace, Your undisturbed calm.

I'm not sure how I get to this place. Too many newscasts with their dire predictions, too many experts telling me to watch out for this, never eat that, stay away from something else. There doesn't seem to be one safe spot on the whole planet. Even at church, there are concerns about building funds and nursery workers and doctrinal controversies.

Lord, I don't want to look at my life through anxious eyes. The world is what it is, but I know that You can give me peace in the midst of it. Right now, I offer all my anxious thoughts to You. I lay them at Your feet. And I ask You to sort through them and nudge me when I need to confront one of them. Until then, I'll relax and rest in Your love and constant watchful care.

Amen.

Man's world has become a nervous one,
encompassed by anxiety.
God's world is other than this; always balanced,
calm, and in order.

Faith Baldwin

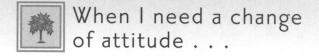

When I need a change of attitude . . .

A relaxed attitude lengthens life.
PROVERBS 14:30 NLT

❧

The Kingdom of God is not a matter of what we eat or drink, but of living a life of goodness and peace and joy in the Holy Spirit. If you serve Christ with this attitude, you will please God.
ROMANS 14:17-18 NLT

❧

May God, who gives this patience and encouragement, help you live in complete harmony with each other— each with the attitude of Christ Jesus toward the other.
ROMANS 15:5 NLT

❧

Be made new in the attitude of your minds; and . . . put on the new self, created to be like God in true righteousness and holiness.
EPHESIANS 4:23-24

❧

The word of God is living and active. . . . It judges the thoughts and attitudes of the heart.
HEBREWS 4:12

. . . I will pray.

Dearest Father,

My life is full of interruption. I can't seem to get one thing finished before someone or something changes the direction of my thoughts and actions. When I awake each morning, my mind is filled with errands, tasks, and duties that need to be done while I catch up on what I didn't get completed the day before.

This morning I find myself sitting squarely in the center of a ferocious bad mood. Lord, I don't like myself this way. I'm sure it's displeasing to You, and my family and friends run for cover when this happens. They can always tell.

That's why I want to take a moment this morning to just sit here in Your presence. Wash away all my irritation, and help me gain a new perspective—one based on a positive, God-filled hope for today rather than a frustrated, negative response to yesterday.

I'm grateful for Your help, Lord. Clear my head and show me how to redeem my time and my attitude as I submit them to You for this moment and every moment of my day.

Amen.

❖

God . . . gives me the freedom to acknowledge
my negative attitudes . . . but not the freedom to act
them out because they are as destructive for me as
they are for the other person.

Rebecca Manley Pippert

When I need help paying my bills . . .

This same God who takes care of me will supply
all your needs from his glorious riches,
which have been given to us in Christ Jesus.
PHILIPPIANS 4:19 NLT

❧

God is able to make all grace (every favor and earthly
blessing) come to you in abundance, so that you may always
and under all circumstances and whatever the need be self-
sufficient [possessing enough to require no aid or support and
furnished in abundance for every good work and charitable
donation].
2 CORINTHIANS 9:8 AMP

❧

A slack hand causes poverty,
but the hand of the diligent makes rich.
PROVERBS 10:4 RSV

❧

You shall remember the LORD your God, for it is he who
gives you power to get wealth; that he may confirm his
covenant which he swore to your fathers, as at this day.
DEUTERONOMY 8:18 RSV

. . . I will pray.

Heavenly Father,

Once again, I sit here looking at a pile of unpaid bills and a beleaguered checkbook, wondering where the money is going to come from. You know how hard we've worked on this, Lord. We've set up a budget, cut back the frills, and even begun to tithe, but this process seems to get only worse instead of better. We really need Your help.

Father, I sure do need Your wisdom. Do I need to get another job? Is there a hole in the bucket that I'm just not seeing? I know it isn't Your will for us to live from month to month barely scraping up enough to keep the bill collectors off our backs.

The only thing I can think to do is turn the whole thing over to You. I lay my hands on this pile of bills and this checkbook and I ask for Your help. Give me the answers I need to get us to a better place financially—even if that means uncomfortable changes. Thank You for being our faithful Provider.

Amen.

❊

Cheer up: birds have bills too,
but they keep on singing.

Author Unknown

When I'm overwhelmed by cares . . .

I will relieve your shoulder of its burden;
I will free your hands from their heavy tasks.
PSALM 81:6 NLT

❧

When the cares of my heart are many,
thy consolations cheer my soul.
PSALM 94:19 RSV

❧

Cast your cares on the LORD
and he will sustain you.
PSALM 55:22

❧

The LORD lifts the burdens of those bent beneath their loads.
PSALM 146:8 NLT

❧

Let him have all your worries and cares, for he is
always thinking about you and watching everything
that concerns you.
1 PETER 5:7 TLB

. . . I will pray.

Precious Lord,

From my window, I see children playing in the yard next door, soaking up the warm air and bright sunshine. I still remember those carefree childhood days, filled with simple pleasures—but that seems so far away now. Instead I feel as though I'm buried under a flood of cares: bills to pay, personality conflicts at work, family disagreements.

My life seems to be buried under an avalanche of responsibilities to be met and problems to be solved. My cares cover me like a cloak, blocking the sunshine from my dreary heart.

Help me lift my head, Lord. Fill me up with Your Spirit. Help me to throw off my cloak of sadness and let in the sunshine of Your love.

As an act of faith, I close my eyes and reach out to You—the Giver and Sustainer of life. I release my cares to You, one by one, piling them high at Your feet. The disappointment at work, the unexpected car repair, my aching joints, and on and on and on . . . until every burden is transferred from my shoulders to Yours.

Thank You for being my Burden-Bearer.

Amen.

❊

Tell God all that is in your heart, as one unloads one's heart, its pleasures and its pains, to a dear friend. Tell Him your troubles, that He may comfort you.

François Fénelon

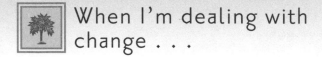

When I'm dealing with change . . .

I am the LORD, I change not.
MALACHI 3:6 KJV

❖

The LORD himself will go before you. He will be with you;
he will not leave you or forget you. Don't be afraid
and don't worry.
DEUTERONOMY 31:8 NCV

❖

[God said]
I'll go ahead of you,
clearing and paving the road.
ISAIAH 45:2 MSG

❖

[The Lord says]
Do not remember the former things,
Nor consider the things of old.
Behold, I will do a new thing,
Now it shall spring forth;
Shall you not know it?
I will even make a road in the wilderness
And rivers in the desert.
ISAIAH 43:18-19 NKJV

. . . I will pray.

Dear Lord,

I know everyone says that change is inevitable—one of the great constants in life—but I just hate it. Even positive change puts a knot in my stomach and fills my mind with anxious thoughts. Why can't things just stay the way they are?

Okay, I guess that doesn't make much sense, but I do need some solution. As ironic as it may seem, I need You to change me. Place a new heart in me, Lord, one that welcomes adventure, appreciates new ways of doing things, and most of all—a heart that places its full and unqualified trust in You.

Lord, I surrender all my misgivings and fears to Your faithful arms. I know as I kneel here before You today that Your only purpose for me is good, in my eternal best interest. Shore up this weakness in me and replace it with Your strength until I no longer cringe at the first sign of change but embrace it as a gift from You. Thank You for dealing with me patiently until my discomfort becomes my new, expanded comfort zone.

Amen.

*

If we try to resist loss and change or to hold on to blessings and joy belonging to a past which must drop away from us, we postpone all the new blessings awaiting us on a higher level.

Hannah Hurnard

When I'm experiencing confusion . . .

[David said]
You are my lamp, O LORD;
The LORD shall enlighten my darkness.
2 SAMUEL 22:29 NKJV

❈

Let him who walks in the dark,
who has no light,
trust in the name of the LORD
and rely on his God.
ISAIAH 50:10

❈

God is not a God of confusion but of peace.
1 CORINTHIANS 14:33 NASB

❈

Lady Wisdom goes to town, stands in a prominent place,
and invites everyone within sound of her voice:
"Are you confused about life, don't know what's going on?
Come with me, oh come, have dinner with me!"
PROVERBS 9:3-4 MSG

. . . I will pray.

Heavenly Father,

My head is screaming—disconnected thoughts swirling around like they've been snatched up in a tornado. I should have come to You sooner—I realize that now. But I kept thinking I could handle it, sort through the clutter and make sense of it all. Why do I fall for that misguided reasoning every time? Now, Lord, You are my hope. Can You fix me?

I'm aware that most of the confusion comes from never really dealing with the issues. I keep picking things up and putting them down again. That must be the recipe for Wandering-Thought Stew because I've really cooked up a batch this time. As I close my eyes, Lord, I'm asking that You help me isolate one thought at a time and pass it along to You. Then I ask that You'll keep all those things for me and bring them up when I'm able to work on them.

You're such a good God. You are the only one in my life who doesn't complain that I'm depending on them too much. In fact, You encourage me to lean on You, for the big things and the small things. I give You thanks, Lord, from my heart.

Amen.

✳

The greatest moments of your life are those when through all the confusion God got a message through to you plain and certain.

Bertha Munro

When I need courage . . .

Be of good courage,
And He shall strengthen your heart,
All you who hope in the Lord.
PSALM 31:24 NKJV

❧

It is impossible for God to lie. Therefore, we who have fled to
him for refuge can take new courage, for we can hold on to his
promise with confidence.
HEBREWS 6:18 NLT

❧

[The Lord said] Have I not commanded you? Be strong and
courageous. Do not be terrified; do not be discouraged, for the
LORD your God will be with you wherever you go.
JOSHUA 1:9

❧

The Holy One, says this: " . . . I refresh the humble and give
new courage to those with repentant hearts."
ISAIAH 57:15 NLT

. . . I will pray.

Mighty God,

I'm afraid—not of anyone or any particular situation, just afraid. I know this isn't pleasing to You, but I can't seem to figure out how to summon my courage and step out into life the way I should. So my family suffers, my work suffers, my friends suffer, and Your will for my life suffers.

The Bible says that if a person needs wisdom, he should ask You for it—maybe the same holds true for courage. It's my only option anyway. I've already tried the human solution—reaching down deep inside myself. You know what I found there—more fear.

So . . . I'm asking, Lord. Give me the courage I need to face my life straight on. I'm sure that will mean conquering one fear at a time as it spills out onto the path in front of me. I'm going to picture You there with me, walking right alongside, and I'm going to remember that when I'm weak, You are strong on my behalf. Thank You for helping me trade in my Cowardly Lion suit for Your mighty armor.

Amen.

�֍

Have plenty of courage. God is stronger than the devil. We are on the winning side.

John Jay Chapman

When I'm struggling with depression . . .

Come quickly, LORD, and answer me,
for my depression deepens.
Don't turn away from me, or I will die.
Let me hear of your unfailing love to me in the morning,
for I am trusting you.
Show me where to walk,
for I have come to you in prayer.
PSALM 143:7-8 NLT

❖

My soul melts from heaviness;
Strengthen me according to Your word.
PSALM 119:28 NKJV

❖

God, Who comforts and encourages and refreshes and
cheers the depressed and the sinking, comforted and
encouraged and refreshed and cheered us.
2 CORINTHIANS 7:6 AMP

❖

When doubts filled my mind,
your comfort gave me renewed hope and cheer.
PSALM 94:19 NLT

. . . I will pray.

Father God,

There is so much in my life today that makes me want to give up. I have no energy to do even the basic things such as getting dressed or taking a shower. Nothing seems right. I despise my job. Food no longer appeals to me. My family and friends want to help me, but the thought of being with anyone is so exhausting.

I just want to be left alone. Why must I feel this way? How could I wake up one day with such despair in my heart? It's not that I haven't struggled to shake off this gloomy cloud. I truly have, but nothing has helped. And then I remember how You died on that cross for me and how alone and abandoned You must have felt.

Thank You for showering me with Your life-giving comfort and the reassurance of knowing that You truly understand my suffering. Lord, I turn to You now in hope and faith because even if everyone else in my life gives up on me, I know You'll hold tight to me with a love that won't let go.

Thank You for always being my Anchor.

Amen.

✤

When you come to the bottom, you find God.

Neville Talbot

When I need to be diligent . . .

The diligent find freedom in their work;
the lazy are oppressed by work.
PROVERBS 12:24 MSG

❖

Easy come, easy go,
but steady diligence pays off.
PROVERBS 13:11 MSG

❖

The diligent obtain precious wealth.
PROVERBS 12:27 NRSV

❖

Lazy men are soon poor; hard workers get rich.
PROVERBS 10:4 TLB

❖

The path of lazy people is overgrown with briers;
the diligent walk down a smooth road.
PROVERBS 15:19 MSG

. . . I will pray.

Precious Lord,

My dog feels it is his job to let me know when someone is walking past our house. He is very attentive toward what he considers to be his watchful duty. Whether it is a jogger, some children riding their bikes, or another dog taking its owner for a walk, my dog does not hesitate to inform me that there's something going on outside. I only wish that I could be so diligent concerning my responsibilities.

My intentions are good, but my enthusiasm rarely matches my objectives. How often I procrastinate and don't finish what I start because it is no longer interesting to me or requires too much energy. Why am I so sluggish about these things?

But You, Father, never slack off or leave things unfinished, and You are always available to help me with what I need to get done. That's a huge relief to me, because it makes me realize that if I follow You with all my heart, You will enable me to finish what I start.

Thank You for prodding me on to becoming a more diligent person.

Amen.

❊

Patience and diligence, like faith, remove mountains.
William Penn

When I'm dealing with disappointment . . .

Unrelenting disappointment leaves you heartsick,
but a sudden good break can turn life around.
PROVERBS 13:12 MSG

❖

Without counsel purposes are disappointed:
but in the multitude of counsellors they are established.
PROVERBS 15:22 KJV

❖

You heard their cries for help and saved them;
they were never disappointed when they sought your aid.
PSALM 22:5 TLB

❖

We know that all things work together for good for those who
love God, who are called according to his purpose.
ROMANS 8:28 NRSV

❖

Why then be downcast? Why be discouraged and sad?
Hope in God! I shall yet praise him again. Yes, I shall again
praise him for his help.
PSALM 42:5 TLB

. . . I will pray.

My Loving Father,

If only I hadn't gotten my hopes up, but I did—and now I feel so disappointed and discouraged. Sometimes I wonder if anything will ever work out for me. Everybody keeps telling me it's just a little bump in the road, but it doesn't feel like a bump to me. It feels as if I've gone off the road completely.

I know I'm probably overreacting, and I also know that I probably wouldn't be feeling this way right now if I had taken time to talk to You about this situation in the beginning. Would You have steered me in another direction? Or allowed me to move ahead for some higher purpose in my life? I'll probably never have the answer to that. The point is that I didn't give You a chance to help me see things from Your perspective.

Lord, take this disappointment I'm feeling and transform it into something positive—a reminder to seek Your guidance; a renewed sense of Your presence with me when things work out and when they don't; and compassion for others when they feel hopeless and disappointed.

Thank You for being the God of second chances.

Amen.

❈

There is no disappointment to those whose wills are buried in the will of God.

Frederick Faber

When I need discernment . . .

The word of God is living and active, sharper than any two-edged sword, piercing to the division of soul and spirit, of joints and marrow, and discerning the thoughts and intentions of the heart.
HEBREWS 4:12 RSV

❖

The discerning heart seeks knowledge, but the mouth of a fool feeds on folly.
PROVERBS 15:14

❖

Test everything. Hold on to the good.
1 THESSALONIANS 5:21

❖

Solid food is for the mature, for those whose faculties have been trained by practice to distinguish good from evil.
HEBREWS 5:14 NRSV

❖

On the lips of the discerning, wisdom is found.
PROVERBS 10:13 NASB

. . . I will pray.

Dear Father of Wisdom,

It's a beautiful morning . . . calm, quiet, yet the television weatherman has warned that a dangerous storm is approaching. One glimpse of the cloudless, periwinkle blue sky makes me believe he is mistaken, but I also realize he has the training, the meteorological instruments, and the understanding that help him assess and see beyond the obvious conditions of the moment.

Father, I also sense an unsettling turbulence concerning a particular situation in my life. Despite the facts and perfect-looking elements, I am discovering that the conditions before me are not as they first appeared. Something feels amiss, like a storm brewing on the distant horizon. I know that discernment is a valuable gift that helps me see with spiritual eyes. Give me a greater understanding of how to use this gift—this instrument and tool that You've provided to help me see clearly and deeply into my situation.

Despite the exterior conditions, open my spiritual understanding and give me the wisdom to assess all that I see and all that is hidden. Help me use it wisely to make the decisions that are in agreement with Your will and plan for my life.

Amen.

❋

A moment's insight is sometimes worth
a life's experience.
Oliver Wendell Holmes

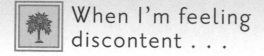

When I'm feeling discontent . . .

Godliness with contentment is great gain.
1 TIMOTHY 6:6

❖

*As for me, my contentment is not in wealth but
in seeing you [Lord] and knowing all is well between us.
And when I awake in heaven, I will be fully satisfied, for
I will see you face to face.*
PSALM 17:15 TLB

❖

*[Jesus said] You're blessed when you're content with just
who you are—no more, no less. That's the moment you find
yourselves proud owners of everything that can't be bought.*
MATTHEW 5:5 MSG

❖

*[Jesus said] If you're content to simply be yourself,
your life will count for plenty.*
MATTHEW 23:12 MSG

❖

I have learned to be content in whatever circumstances I am.
PHILIPPIANS 4:11 NASB

. . . I will pray.

Dear God,

I've been wondering lately why I feel so unhappy with my life. Nothing moves or inspires me. I don't like feeling bored with life in general—especially since Your Word says to be content in all things and anxious about nothing.

But how do I get there? It sure isn't by looking at the people around me. They are all scurrying back and forth, trying to accumulate enough possessions, make enough money, recapture enough of their youth to satisfy their inner longings. At least I know those things aren't the answer. I don't want the world's recipe for contentment, Lord—fragile, temporary, superficial. I want Your recipe for inner, not just outer, peace.

Too often I have relied on my own abilities and accomplishments for happiness and contentment. Help me lay down my own efforts and seek Your plan for my life. Help me to dream again and set new goals, knowing You will be there to accomplish my heart's desires.

Deep down, I know that a contented life comes from a contented heart and sense of purpose. Infuse my life and heart with Your purpose, and help me to find contentment in knowing You are my Partner in all things worthwhile.

Amen.

❋

Purpose is what gives life a meaning.
. . . A drifting boat always drifts downstream.
Charles H. Parkhurst

When I'm dealing with discouragement . . .

Let all who are discouraged take heart.
Let us praise the Lord together, and exalt his name.
PSALM 34:2-3 TLB

❧

Be encouraged, you who worship God.
The LORD listens to those in need.
PSALM 69:32-33 NCV

❧

When I pray, you answer me;
you encourage me by giving me the strength I need.
PSALM 138:3 NLT

❧

O my soul, don't be discouraged.
Don't be upset. Expect God to act!
For I know that I shall again have plenty of reason to praise
him for all that he will do. He is my help! He is my God!
PSALM 42:11 TLB

. . . I will pray.

Dear Lord of Promise,

I've given my all in this situation. I've tried my best to do what is right and noble and pleasing to You. And yet, I don't recall a time when I have ever felt so discouraged and more like giving up. I need Your help, Lord.

I've never been a negative person. I have tried to see the best in all things and all people, and even in all situations. I remind myself during times of discouragement that even David had to encourage himself in order to keep his attitude and faith intact.

You, Lord, have always been my constant in life—my North Star that has kept me focused and anchored in hope. Shine Your light upon my heart and spirit and help me find my way through this time of discouragement. Remind me that there is nothing too big for You to handle and that, just like the bulbs planted in the darkness of winter, new life will spring forth when winter is over. Bring springtime to my soul, Lord. Water my discouraged and despairing heart with Your Word, and encourage me with Your promise of hope.

Amen.

❉

Every step toward Christ kills a doubt.
Every thought, word and deed for Him carries you
away from discouragement.

Theodore Ledyard Cuyler

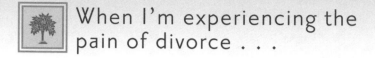

When I'm experiencing the pain of divorce . . .

He heals the brokenhearted, binding up their wounds.
PSALM 147:3 TLB

✤

"Don't be afraid, because you will not be ashamed.
Don't be embarrassed, because you will not be disgraced.
You will forget the shame you felt earlier;
You will not remember the shame you felt when
you lost your husband.
The God who made you is like your husband.
His name is the LORD All-Powerful.
The Holy One of Israel is the one who saves you.
He is called the God of all the earth.
You were like a woman whose husband left her,
and you were very sad.
You were like a wife who married young
and then her husband left her.
But the LORD called you to be his,"
says your God.
ISAIAH 54:4-6 NCV

✤

I am overcome with joy because of your unfailing love,
for you have seen my troubles,
and you care about the anguish of my soul.
PSALM 31:7 NLT

. . . I will pray.

Heavenly Father,

I'm not sure what went wrong with my marriage. I wish we could have worked things out. There are times when my mind is filled with questions. Should I have fought harder? Did I give up too soon? What could I have done differently?

I know that divorce is never one person's fault. I don't want to play the blame game anymore. More than anything, I need to feel Your presence and power and love in my life. I know that You are strong when I am weak. Take my weakness, my sadness, and my disappointment and show me how to lean into Your strength. Bring healing to my heart and to the hearts of all who are affected by this divorce. I surrender my pain to You. Take away any bitterness that has found its way to my heart and replace it with genuine forgiveness.

Lord, I look to You for my life from here. In the natural, my future looks uncertain. But I'm confident that You have a new path for me—one that I could neither ask for or even imagine. I'm looking forward to making a new start with You leading the way.

Amen.

✳

Failure and the evil inherent in divorce would destroy us were it not for the fact that God keeps His promises and continues to love even when we break our promises and our love fails.

William H. Willimon

When I have doubts . . .

Jesus said to him, "If you can believe, all things are possible to him who believes." Immediately the father of the child cried out and said with tears, "Lord, I believe; help my unbelief!"

MARK 9:23-24 NKJV

❋

Let your roots grow down into him and draw up nourishment from him, so you will grow in faith, strong and vigorous in the truth you were taught.

COLOSSIANS 2:7 NLT

❋

[Jesus said] Do not fear, only believe.

MARK 5:36 RSV

❋

[Jesus said] Have faith in God. Truly I tell you, if you say to this mountain, "Be taken up and thrown into the sea," and if you do not doubt in your heart, but believe that what you say will come to pass, it will be done for you. So I tell you, whatever you ask for in prayer, believe that you have received it, and it will be yours.

MARK 11:22-24 NRSV

. . . I will pray.

Loving Lord,

I'm at a crossroads in my life. I want to believe in You completely, wholeheartedly, devoutly, but doubts plague my heart and mind. Are You really there? If You are, how can You possibly love a person like me? Others in my life have disappointed me—will You disappoint me too?

Despite my doubts, Lord, I've seen You working, intervening in my circumstances. I've felt Your soft touch around the corners of my heart. I've sensed Your presence. Somehow deep inside, I know You're real. In a way, that makes the doubting seem so much worse.

Today, Lord, I surrender my doubting heart and mind to You. I ask You to shore up the unstable timbers and wash away the remnants of past heartaches. I know that without Your help, I'll never be able to stay on the path of truth. But with Your help, Lord, I hope to become all You created me to be—a person of faith and power, a person who holds on to You and accomplishes Your perfect plan. I believe, Lord. Help me to believe more.

Amen.

Where reason cannot wade, there faith may swim.

Thomas Watson

When I need endurance . . .

*[Jesus said] In the good soil, these are the ones who,
when they hear the word, hold it fast in an honest and good
heart, and bear fruit with patient endurance.*
LUKE 8:15 NRSV

❖

*We pray that you'll have the strength to stick it out
over the long haul—not the grim strength of gritting your
teeth but the glory-strength God gives. It is strength that
endures the unendurable and spills over into joy, thanking
the Father who makes us strong enough to take part in
everything bright and beautiful that he has for us.*
COLOSSIANS 1:11-12 MSG

❖

The one who endures to the end will be saved.
MATTHEW 10:22 NRSV

❖

*In our trouble God has comforted us—and this, too, to help
you: to show you from our personal experience how God will
tenderly comfort you when you undergo these same sufferings.
He will give you the strength to endure.*
2 CORINTHIANS 1:6-7 TLB

. . . I will pray.

Heavenly Father,

I've been thinking about that movie, Titanic, where that man—I think his name was Jack—saves a woman from slipping over the edge by grabbing hold of her hand and telling her, "I won't let go." Throughout the movie he demonstrates that same kind of tenacity in the face of great odds. Even when he was dying, he was determined not to let go.

That's the kind of endurance I need to win against this trial that has invaded my life. I have to hold on, keep my promise, and stay the course. I can't let my commitment slip—not even for a moment. No matter how hard it gets, I can't quit. I have to keep walking. I can't let go.

Heavenly Father, I am depending on You to be the Light in my darkest hours, to be my Strength when my own has failed, and to fill me with tireless endurance as I make my way to the other side of this situation. Through it all, Lord, I know that I can make it. I can keep holding on—because You will never let go of me!

Amen.

✳

Nothing great was ever done without much enduring.

Catherine of Siena

When I'm being harassed by my enemies . . .

You [Lord] prepare a table before me
in the presence of my enemies.
PSALM 23:5 NKJV

❧

[The Lord] delivered me from my strong enemy,
from those who hated me—I who was helpless in their hands.
On the day when I was weakest, they attacked. But the Lord
held me steady. He led me to a place of safety, for he delights
in me.
PSALM 18:17-19 TLB

❧

Do not be terrified, or afraid of them. The LORD your God,
who goes before you, He will fight for you.
DEUTERONOMY 1:29-30 NKJV

❧

The LORD your God is going with you! He will fight for you
against your enemies, and he will give you victory!
DEUTERONOMY 20:4 NLT

❧

Do not take revenge. . . . "It is mine to avenge;
I will repay," says the Lord.
ROMANS 12:19

. . . I will pray.

Dear God,

I remember as a child hearing a schoolmate tell another that his dad was big and would fight for him. Soon an argument ensued between the two boys about whose dad was the strongest, tallest, and had the most muscles. Each of them stood his ground, confidently trusting in his father's strength. They never fought each other but left the real challenge up to the ones they knew could and would take up for them. Relying on the strength of their dads helped them face each other and transform their fear into courage.

Sometimes life feels like a battlefield. It isn't easy to walk in enemy territory and face the intentions of those who try to harass me, but I also know I do not face my enemies alone.

Dear God, I know that life's bullies will always be around. Help me remember that no matter what they throw at me, You are on my side. Help me to also remember that You are only a prayer away and always ready and willing to fight for me. Thank You, God, for being the only hero I'll ever need in the presence of my enemies.

Amen.

❊

It is infinitely better to have the whole world for
our enemies and God for our friend, than to have the
whole world for our friends and God for our enemy.

John Brown

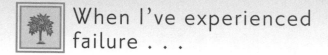

When I've experienced failure . . .

I let it all out;
I said, "I'll make a clean breast of my failures to GOD."
Suddenly the pressure was gone—my guilt dissolved,
my sin disappeared.

PSALM 32:5 MSG

❊

I am waiting for you, O LORD.
You must answer for me, O Lord my God.
I prayed, "Don't let my enemies gloat over me
or rejoice at my downfall."

PSALM 38:15-16 NLT

❊

You know me inside and out, you hold me together,
you never fail to stand me tall in your presence
so I can look you in the eye.

PSALM 41:12 MSG

❊

And we know that God causes all things to work together
for good to those who love God, to those who are called
according to His purpose.

ROMANS 8:28 NASB

. . . I will pray.

Gracious Lord,

I've been remembering that first cake I baked—You know, the one where I left out the sugar. I'm still not sure how I missed such an important ingredient. It even looked great when it came out of the oven, lightly browned and smelling like heaven. The icing went on so smoothly. But one bite and everyone knew—the whole thing had to go into the trash.

I've had plenty of failures since the day I baked that cake, Lord. But the one today felt really bad—kind of like with the cake. I could just smell success. I planned and executed everything so carefully—and then one little oversight ruined everything.

Help me remember that this situation is not a permanent part of my life. Give me a teachable spirit that I might learn from my mistakes those things that will help me in the future. Thank You for reminding me that I've made many wonderful cakes since that first failed one. Help me remember that failure is never final.

Amen.

✻

A failure is not someone who has tried and failed;
it is someone who has given up trying and
resigned himself to failure;
it is not a condition, but an attitude.

Sydney J. Harris

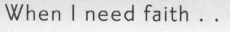

When I need faith . . .

*What is faith? It is the confident assurance that what
we hope for is going to happen. It is the evidence of things we
cannot yet see.*
HEBREWS 11:1 NLT

✽

We walk by faith, not by sight.
2 CORINTHIANS 5:7 NASB

✽

*[Jesus said] If you have faith as a grain of mustard seed,
you will say to this mountain, "Move from here to there," and
it will move; and nothing will be impossible to you.*
MATTHEW 17:20 RSV

✽

*Your faith is growing more and more, and the love that every
one of you has for each other is increasing.*
2 THESSALONIANS 1:3 NCV

✽

*None of those who have faith in God
will ever be disgraced for trusting him.*
PSALM 25:3 TLB

. . . I will pray.

Dear God,

Your Word reminds me that childlike faith is powerful. Children believe without reserve or hesitation. I remember jumping as a child from a diving board into the waiting, outstretched arms of my father, knowing I could trust him to catch me. I need that kind of faith again, dear Father—the kind of faith that believes You are watching me and waiting with outstretched arms to carry me through this trial.

It's easy to praise You after I've reached the other side of a challenge, but the kind of faith I long for is simple, childlike faith that will praise You before the victory is won, before I leap into the unknown, before I see the waters parted and dry ground revealed, before I experience the tangible evidence of Your provision.

I'm remembering the promise from Your Word that says if I have faith the size of a tiny mustard seed, I can speak to mountains and they'll be removed. Help my faith to find its voice and praise You in advance for Your answer.

Amen.

❋

Faith does not mean believing without evidence.
It means believing in realities that go beyond sense
and sight—for which a totally different sort of
evidence is required.

John Baillie

When I need assurance of God's favor . . .

I entreated Your favor with my whole heart;
Be merciful to me according to Your word.
PSALM 119:58 NKJV

❄

Let your favor shine on your servant.
In your unfailing love, save me.
Don't let me be disgraced, O LORD.
PSALM 31:16-17 NLT

❄

Let the Lord our God favor us and give us success.
PSALM 90:17 TLB

❄

His anger is but for a moment,
His favor is for a lifetime.
PSALM 30:5 NASB

❄

Keep me as the apple of your eye.
PSALM 17:8

. . . I will pray.

Precious Lord,

I stand in awe of Your majesty and all that You have created. Your mighty hand turns the tide of the oceans and is able to calm raging seas. You change and rearrange whatever is needed to accomplish Your will in the world and in the lives of Your children. You are a God who rules the universe and names each star that You set against an ebony sky. At the same time, You care enough to reach down and smooth out the path before me.

Your favor in my life is unearned—I just want You to know I understand that. It's part of the gift package Jesus paid for on the cross, literally one blessing after another, beginning with my salvation and encompassing so many smaller miracles—stuff that has Your name written all over it.

I don't feel deserving of such unmerited favor, but I've learned that Your favor is a direct result of Your wondrous grace. Help me to move forward with confidence, knowing Your hand of favor is upon me today and every day of my life.

Amen.

Measure not God's love and favor by your own feeling. The sun shines as clearly in the darkest day as it does in the brightest. The difference is not in the sun, but in some clouds.

Richard Sibbs

When I'm dealing with fear . . .

I, the LORD your God, hold your right hand;
it is I who say to you, "Fear not, I will help you."
ISAIAH 41:13 RSV

❖

God hath not given us the spirit of fear; but of power,
and of love, and of a sound mind.
2 TIMOTHY 1:7 KJV

❖

Fear not, for I am with you,
be not dismayed, for I am your God;
I will strengthen you, I will help you,
I will uphold you with my victorious right hand.
ISAIAH 41:10 RSV

❖

[Jesus said] Peace I leave with you; my peace I give you.
I do not give to you as the world gives. Do not let your
hearts be troubled and do not be afraid.
JOHN 14:27

. . . I will pray.

Heavenly Father,

I feel as if I'm slowly being paralyzed by fear—not just my actions but even my thoughts. I know that the opposite of fear is faith, but right now my faith feels powerless, immobile, and stuck in the muck and mire of what looks like a hopeless situation.

David didn't seem to be fearful at all as he ran to kill the giant Goliath. I need the kind of giant-conquering courage David possessed, regardless of his feelings, his fear, and the challenge he faced. Even Goliath considered the odds and David's size and then laughed at David's feeble attempt to bring him down. But David knew that with You by his side, he could slay any giant he faced.

Father, give me fearless faith that steps forward with courage. Help me remember that just as You were with David in the midst of his battle, You are also with me. With You, nothing is unconquerable, even fear itself. Thank You for walking beside and before me in every battle, assuring me I need not fear the giants in my life.

Amen.

✤

God incarnate is the end of fear;
and the heart that realizes that He is in the midst . . .
will be quiet in the midst of alarm.

F. B. Meyer

When I need to forgive . . .

*Peter came to [Jesus] and asked, "Lord, how often should
I forgive someone who sins against me? Seven times?"
"No!" Jesus replied, "seventy times seven!"*
MATTHEW 18:21-22 NLT

❊

*Get along with each other, and forgive each other.
If someone does wrong to you, forgive that person because
the Lord forgave you.*
COLOSSIANS 3:13 NCV

❊

*[Jesus said] Judge not, and you will not be judged;
condemn not, and you will not be condemned; forgive,
and you will be forgiven.*
LUKE 6:37 RSV

❊

*[Jesus said] Whenever you stand praying, forgive, if you have
anything against anyone, so that your Father who is in
heaven will also forgive you your transgressions. But if you do
not forgive, neither will your Father who is in heaven forgive
your transgressions.*
MARK 11:25-26 NASB

. . . I will pray.

Dear Father,

I don't know where I would be today without Your forgiveness. I don't want to think about what my life might be like if You had not picked me up and planted my feet on the solid ground of Your love. I'll never forget the moment the revelation of Your forgiveness settled into my heart. I didn't deserve such love or such grace, but I knew the moment I asked for forgiveness, You washed away the old and unsatisfying dregs of sin that had filled my heart and soul. Suddenly, I felt free from my past, my guilt, my shame, and my feelings of unworthiness.

Like an old, tarnished cup made shiny and bright after being dipped into a cleaning solution, Your forgiveness felt like liquid love being poured upon my head and down into my heart. Father, help me to forgive with the same measure of forgiveness You have afforded me—complete and unqualified. Fill my heart with unconditional love that looks past the imperfections of others.

It isn't always easy to forgive, but I trust You to give me a heart like Yours—a heart that, empowered by love, forgives easily, quickly, and completely.

Amen.

❋

Humanity is never so beautiful as when praying for forgiveness or else forgiving another.

Jean Paul Richter

When I need help identifying my gifts . . .

We are God's [own] handiwork (His workmanship),
recreated in Christ Jesus, . . . that we may do those good
works which God predestined (planned beforehand) for us
[taking paths which He prepared ahead of time],
that we should walk in them.

EPHESIANS 2:10 AMP

❖

You created my inmost being;
you knit me together in my mother's womb.
I praise you because I am fearfully and wonderfully made;
your works are wonderful, I know that full well.

PSALM 139:13-14

❖

Each of us was given grace according to the measure of
Christ's gift. Therefore it is said, "When he ascended on high
he made captivity itself a captive; he gave gifts to his people."

EPHESIANS 4:7-8 NRSV

❖

And I am convinced and sure of this very thing,
that He Who began a good work in you will continue until
the day of Jesus Christ [right up to the time of His return],
developing [that good work] and perfecting and bringing it
to full completion in you.

PHILIPPIANS 1:6 AMP

. . . I will pray.

Dear God,

When an artist takes up his brush to paint, one stroke of color sets his gift into motion. One note of a psalmist's anthem births a song, and with a writer's first transcribed word, a story finds its voice.

Dear God, I don't know how to identify and determine my gifts, but I am ready and willing to unwrap the gift You have placed inside me and take that first step toward developing it to the best of my ability.

All gifts have a beginning, even if they are small in nature. Without realizing it, I have allowed my gifts to lie dormant inside me, feeling they were inadequate and small compared to the gifts I see in others. Help me realize that my gift is a tool in my hand, given by You to help me fulfill my purpose in life. Help me to dig down into the treasure chest of my heart and find my passion—what motivates me to action—what moves me with compassion—what comes easily and naturally and flows from my soul.

Amen.

God gives to every man the virtue, temper, understanding, taste, that lifts him into life, and lets him fall just in the niche he was ordained to fill.

William Cowper

When I need help pursuing my goals . . .

You know that in a race all the runners run, but only one gets the prize. So run to win! All those who compete in the games use self-control so they can win a crown. That crown is an earthly thing that lasts only a short time, but our crown will never be destroyed. So I do not run without a goal.

1 CORINTHIANS 9:24-26 NCV

Since we are surrounded by such a great cloud of witnesses, let us throw off everything that hinders and the sin that so easily entangles, and let us run with perseverance the race marked out for us. Let us fix our eyes on Jesus, the author and perfecter of our faith, who for the joy set before him endured the cross.

HEBREWS 12:1-2

Record the vision
And inscribe it on tablets,
That the one who reads it may run.
For the vision is yet for the appointed time;
It hastens toward the goal and it will not fail.

HABAKKUK 2:2-3 NASB

. . . I will pray.

Dear God,

My goals have sat on the back burner of my life for a very long time. Maybe I've talked myself into believing I can never fit them into my already busy schedule. Or . . . maybe I've convinced myself that if I never begin pursuing my goals, I won't have to worry about the perseverance and energy they will require, or even the possibility of failure.

God, I admit that I have used one excuse after another for not pursuing my goals. I have overused the word "someday" to the point of the ridiculous. But as the days, months, and years pass by, I am realizing that today is yesterday's "someday." If I ever truly hope to reach my goals, I need to pull them from the back burner and map out a winning plan of pursuit—starting today, starting now.

I know that all things are possible when I depend on Your strength and guidance. I ask You to be my Partner and show me how to set a determined path and plan for reaching my goals.

Amen.

❋

A written-down goal, in some way no one yet understands, tends to attract every ingredient it needs to realize it.

Author Unknown

When I need help understanding God's will . . .

As your plan unfolds, even the simple can understand it.
PSALM 119:130 TLB

❄

*David said, "All these plans were written with
the LORD guiding me. He helped me understand
everything in the plans."*
1 CHRONICLES 28:19 NCV

❄

*[Not in your own strength] for it is God Who is all the while
effectually at work in you [energizing and creating in you the
power and desire], both to will and to work for His good
pleasure and satisfaction and delight.*
PHILIPPIANS 2:13 AMP

❄

*"I know what I am planning for you," says the LORD.
"I have good plans for you, not plans to hurt you.
I will give you hope and a good future."*
JEREMIAH 29:11 NCV

. . . I will pray.

Dear God,

Sometimes my life feels like a jigsaw puzzle with many tiny fragments waiting to be picked up and put into their proper places. Every now and then, I capture a glimpse of what I think the puzzle may look like, but I long to see the finished picture and how every piece fits perfectly together.

Dear God, help me trust You and know that You are the Master Designer of my life—the one who created the pieces and the one who sets them all in place. As my life unfolds day by day, fill me with faith and assurance that I am in the center of Your will, even when I don't see my destiny clearly. If I intentionally or unintentionally try to pick up the pieces and make them fit my own agenda, help me remember that Your design is the only one that will result in what's right for my life in accordance with Your will.

Help me, dear God, to trust You with every fragment of my life, knowing You will fit each piece of my life into the bigger picture of Your will for me.

Amen.

❋

When we seek first the kingdom of God and
righteousness, fulfillment comes as a by-product. . . .
That satisfaction is better than we ever imagined.
God can make the pieces of this world's puzzle fit
together; He helps us view the world from
a new perspective.

Erwin W. Lutzer

When I need help under-standing God's Word . . .

Give me understanding, that I may observe Your law
And keep it with all my heart.
PSALM 119:34 NASB

❈

If you want better insight and discernment, and are searching
for them as you would for lost money or hidden treasure, then
wisdom will be given you, and knowledge of God himself; you
will soon learn the importance of reverence for the Lord and
of trusting him. For the Lord grants wisdom! His every word
is a treasure of knowledge and understanding.
PROVERBS 2:3-6 TLB

❈

Lead me in Your truth and teach me.
PSALM 25:5 NASB

❈

Your word is a lamp to my feet
and a light for my path.
PSALM 119:105

. . . I will pray.

Faithful Lord,

When a ferocious storm knocked out all the electrical power in my home and I searched desperately in the darkness for a flashlight and batteries, I was reminded that life's storms will also find me stumbling aimlessly through the dark if I don't keep the light and security of Your Word burning brightly in my heart.

Words alone are like a flashlight with no batteries. The flashlight is powerless to shine into the darkness without them. Faithful Lord, as I open the pages of Your inspired Word, charge me with spiritual insight and help me gain heart and not just head knowledge. Shine the light of Your Word upon my paths of darkness. Prepare me for the storms of life before they occur. Teach me and help me understand what You have written to me. When I search for answers, teach me to seek out Your instruction, Your guidance, and Your counsel first.

What a difference a flashlight with batteries makes when riding out the storms of life. What a difference Your written Word, charged with understanding, makes when I need to find my way in the darkness. Thank You for helping me keep the batteries of my heart fully charged.

Amen.

❈

Come, Holy Ghost, for moved by thee
The prophets wrote and spoke;
Unlock the truth, thyself the key,
Unseal the sacred book.

John Calvin

When I'm experiencing grief . . .

[The Lord] was despised and rejected by men;
a man of sorrows, and acquainted with grief. . . .
Surely he has borne our griefs
and carried our sorrows.
ISAIAH 53:3-4 RSV

❖

Jesus said, "Truly, truly, I say to you, that you will weep and
lament, . . . but your grief will be turned into joy."
JOHN 16:20 NASB

❖

I say, "It is my grief
that the right hand of the Most High has changed."
I will call to mind the deeds of the LORD;
yea, I will remember thy wonders of old.
I will meditate on all thy work,
and muse on thy mighty deeds.
PSALM 77:10-12 RSV

❖

Have mercy on me, LORD, for I am in distress.
My sight is blurred because of my tears.
My body and soul are withering away.
PSALM 31:9 NLT

. . . I will pray.

Gracious Father,

What do I do with this grief? I can't pray it away, shop it away, cry it away, or talk it away. It stays constant in my thoughts, heavy in my heart. I have no place to run with this heartache except to You. I read in Your Word that You were a Man of sorrows, that You also know what grief feels like. That's why I'm sure You understand the deep pangs of despair that keep washing over me.

I reach out to You in faith, Father, praying that You will hear the cries of my breaking heart and bring comfort to me. Each day, I will depend on You to help me take one more step toward healing. Restore my soul and walk with me through this valley. I trust You, gentle Shepherd, to make Your presence known. Give me hope that I will smile and experience joy once more.

Lord, I know life for me will never be the same—but I cling to Your promise that one day I will be able to once again embrace the life You've given me.

Amen.

❊

Grief can be your servant,
helping you to feel more compassion
for others who hurt.

Robert Harold Schuller

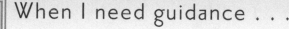

When I need guidance . . .

The LORD says, "I will guide you along the best pathway for
your life. I will advise you and watch over you."
PSALM 32:8 NLT

❋

He leadeth me in the paths of righteousness
for his name's sake.
PSALM 23:3 KJV

❋

Teach me your way, O LORD;
lead me in a straight path.
PSALM 27:11

❋

We humans keep brainstorming options and plans,
but GOD'S purpose prevails.
PROVERBS 19:21 MSG

❋

If you leave God's paths and go astray, you will hear a Voice
behind you say, "No, this is the way; walk here."
ISAIAH 30:21 TLB

. . . I will pray.

Dear God,

The way before me is too steep, too jagged, too dark, and too uncertain. I don't plan to take one more step until You show me which path to take. I have felt my way through many difficult situations, but this one is different. As a sailor needs a reliable compass to know where he is going, I need the compass of Your guiding light. Order my thoughts as I search Your Word and then listen for Your voice. Clear the pathway before me and give me patience as I wait for You to show me my next step.

Just as mountaineers climb slowly upward toward their destination, careful to place each foot on solid rock, guide me one step at a time as Your plan unfolds before me. Only You can secure my footing and keep me from slipping.

I place all of my trust in You, dear God, to be my guiding Light and my solid Rock of protection. I won't begin this journey until I hear from You. Waiting is tough, but I know it will be worth it long before I reach my destination.

Amen.

❖

Abraham did not know the way,
but he knew the Guide.

Lee Roberson

When I'm searching for happiness . . .

LORD, *you have made me happy by what you have done;*
I will sing for joy about what your hands have done.
PSALM 92:4 NCV

❖

You have made known to me the path of life;
you will fill me with joy in your presence,
with eternal pleasures at your right hand.
PSALM 16:11

❖

Taste and see that the LORD is good.
Oh, the joys of those who trust in him!
PSALM 34:8 NLT

❖

Happy are those who trust in the LORD.
PROVERBS 16:20 NRSV

❖

Oh, the joy of drinking deeply from the Fountain of Salvation!
ISAIAH 12:3 TLB

. . . I will pray.

Precious Lord,

Sometimes I close my eyes and daydream about the way I wish my life could be. I wonder if a new car, a new house, a closet full of new clothes, or moving to a new—more exciting—location would make my life easier, more restful, and happier. When I open my eyes, I realize that many of my dreams are nothing more than impossibilities—fool's gold that tempts me into believing new arrangements or new possessions will finally bring me the kind of happiness I seek. In reality, I'm not at all sure how to search for real happiness.

In my quest for bliss, help me to see the difference between the short-lived and temporary fixes and the deep, abiding kind of happiness that can occupy my heart despite my circumstances. Help me define my life by the joys of meaningful relationships rather than possessions. Show me the priceless treasures within my own heart that can't be bought or sold. Wrap me in the joy of Your presence and teach me to dance throughout my life with gratitude and delight. Only then will I be truly happy.

Amen.

❉

God cannot give us happiness and peace apart
from Himself, because it is not there.
There is no such thing.

C. S. Lewis

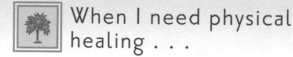

When I need physical healing . . .

You shall serve the LORD your God,
and He will bless your bread and your water.
And I will take sickness away from the midst of you.
EXODUS 23:25 NKJV

❖

I am the LORD who heals you.
EXODUS 15:26 NLT

❖

Heal me, O LORD, and I shall be healed; save me,
and I shall be saved.
JEREMIAH 17:14 KJV

❖

They cried to the LORD in their trouble,
and he saved them from their distress;
he sent out his word and healed them.
PSALM 107:19-20 NRSV

❖

He took the punishment, and that made us whole.
Through his bruises we get healed.
ISAIAH 53:5 MSG

. . . I will pray.

Merciful Father,

Life has changed. Every moment, I wait with expectation for You to touch me, heal me, and raise me from this bed of affliction. I admit that I am vulnerable and desperate for Your touch on my physical body.

As prayers ascend to Your throne on my behalf from those I love, I've never felt more thankful for this gift of life. When You died for me on the cross, You died so that I can live. You were beaten by those who didn't understand who You were. The stripes You bore paid a price for my healing today.

When I am broken, I believe that You can fix me. When I am weak, I believe I can rest in Your strength. Bring wholeness to my body, the temple of Your Spirit, and restore health to me again. Lead me to the earthly solutions that will help me get well and stay healthy. By faith, I ask You to make me well. And I thank You in advance for Your healing touch.

Amen.

❋

No one ever looks in vain to the Great Physician.

F. F. Bosworth

When I need emotional healing . . .

Weeping may endure for a night,
but joy cometh in the morning.
PSALM 30:5 KJV

❖

He will wipe away every tear from their eyes;
and there will no longer be any death;
there will no longer be any mourning, or crying, or pain.
REVELATION 21:4 NASB

❖

God blesses those who are kind to the poor. . . . He nurses
them when they are sick, and soothes their pains and worries.
PSALM 41:1,3 TLB

❖

He will not break the bruised reed, nor quench the
dimly burning flame. He will encourage the fainthearted,
those tempted to despair.
ISAIAH 42:3 TLB

❖

Those who discover these words live, really live;
body and soul, they're bursting with health.
PROVERBS 4:22 MSG

. . . I will pray.

Dear Heavenly Father,

The rose-colored glasses are gone. I cannot pretend that my heart is not broken. Physically and spiritually, I am okay, but emotionally, I feel as if I have been ambushed. I always thought I could keep my emotions in check if I looked at everything from a spiritual viewpoint. But I am finding as I mature in life that emotions are what make us human and real—and even vulnerable. Without them, life would be pretty dull. It's just so hard when I hurt so deeply and for such a prolonged time.

Dear Father, You created my emotions—those that make me laugh and those that also bring pain. Thank You for providing a release of that pain through tears and a healing touch to my parched heart.

I'm thankful that You care about my hurts and disappointments. As my first step of healing, I enter Your emergency room and ask You to pour Your soothing balm of love across my wounded heart.

Amen.

Psychotherapy will put a Band-Aid on the gash;
but for healing, men's lives must be
changed from within.

Raymond J. Larson

When I'm dealing with a sense of helplessness . . .

GOD *takes the side of the helpless;*
when I was at the end of my rope, he saved me.
PSALM 116:6 MSG

❧

You have been a defense for the helpless,
A defense for the needy in his distress.
ISAIAH 25:4 NASB

❧

Lord, because I am poor and helpless, please remember me.
You are my helper and savior. My God, do not wait.
PSALM 40:17 NCV

❧

Moses said to the people, "Do not be afraid. Stand still,
and see the salvation of the LORD, which He will
accomplish for you today."
EXODUS 14:13 NKJV

❧

The LORD is my strength and my shield;
My heart trusts in Him, and I am helped;
Therefore my heart exults,
And with my song I shall thank Him.
PSALM 28:7 NASB

. . . I will pray.

Dear God,

I've always prided myself on being a strong person, one who is able to cope with problems confidently and aggressively. This problem is different. I feel as if my hands are tied behind my back. I sense that if I tried to do anything, I would fall on my face. Could it be that my sense of helplessness is really a message to take my hands off this situation?

As I pray about what to do, I'm reminded of the scripture that tells me to be still. That's a tough assignment for someone who is used to helping and solving problems. Help me to understand that being still while I wait for You to act is not a sign of helplessness but rather of total trust in You. As a caterpillar waits silently in the cocoon to develop into a butterfly, it is making progress in the inactivity and stillness.

Dear God, please turn my feelings of helplessness into a resting place in You as I wait for Your instruction to move or be still.

Amen.

❖

One of the ways that our faith expresses itself is by our ability to be still, to be present, and not to panic or lose perspective. God still does His best work in the most difficult of circumstances.

Tim Hansel

When I need hope . . .

Why are you cast down, O my soul,
and why are you disquieted within me?
Hope in God; for I shall again praise him,
my help and my God.

PSALM 43:5 RSV

❧

May the God of hope fill you with all joy and
peace in believing, so that you will abound in hope by the
power of the Holy Spirit.

ROMANS 15:13 NASB

❧

I would have lost heart, unless I had believed
That I would see the goodness of the LORD
In the land of the living.

PSALM 27:13 NKJV

❧

Save me from my enemies, GOD—
you're my only hope!

PSALM 143:9 MSG

. . . I will pray.

Precious Lord,

In the past when there were no answers for my situation and I had no place to turn, You brought hope to my wilderness. Remembering those times of hopelessness and how You brought me through them gives me hope for what I am facing now.

The Bible says that Your ways are past finding out! I could never have imagined how You would work out every detail of the trials I've faced. You never do things halfway. You are a God of completion and wholeness.

When You led the children of Israel through the wilderness, You were faithful to meet all of their needs. You provided a cloud by day to keep them safe from the scorching desert heat and a fire by night to keep them warm. You fed them perfect food—angels' food, heavenly manna—every morning. None of their needs went unnoticed by You. Just as You provided fresh manna and daily hope in a barren desert for them, my every need is bathed in hope and the promise of Your provision.

Amen.

✳

O God, our help in ages past,
Our hope for years to come,
Our shelter from the stormy blast,
And our eternal home.

Isaac Watts

When I need a job . . .

*Let the thief no longer steal, but rather let him labor,
doing honest work with his hands, so that he may be
able to give to those in need.*
 EPHESIANS 4:28 RSV

❧

*Every man who eats and drinks sees good in all his labor
—it is the gift of God.*
ECCLESIASTES 3:13 NASB

❧

*You will eat the fruit of your labor;
blessings and prosperity will be yours.*
PSALM 128:2

❧

*It is good and fitting for one to eat and drink, and to enjoy
the good of all his labor in which he toils under the sun all the
days of his life which God gives him; for it is his heritage. As
for every man to whom God has given riches and wealth, and
given him power to eat of it, to receive his heritage and rejoice
in his labor—this is the gift of God.*
ECCLESIASTES 5:18-19 NKJV

. . . I will pray.

Heavenly Father,

Before I even ask, You are aware of my need for employment. I don't even have to wonder if it is Your will that I work. You have given me two good hands, two good feet, and all of the skills I need to help my family and myself financially. I'm not sure what the market will look like or how many jobs will be available in my field, but I do know that You will lead me to the very job You've prepared for me—a job that is suited to my physical, spiritual, and mental needs and abilities.

I pray in advance for my future employers and for their needs to be met in some way through my qualifications and association with them. Help me to be a blessing in the job that You have in mind for me. Please provide a place to work where I can grow as a person, thrive financially, and fulfill my potential and Your will in my life.

As doors open, help me know which ones to walk through. Confirm Your provision as I step into the right position and place of employment.

Amen.

✤

Each individual has his own kind of living assigned to him by the Lord as a sort of sentry post.

John Calvin

When I want to know God better . . .

I want to know Christ and the power of his resurrection and the fellowship of sharing in his sufferings, becoming like him in his death, and so, somehow, to attain to the resurrection from the dead.

PHILIPPIANS 3:10-11

❈

[Jesus said] This is eternal life: [it means] to know (to perceive, recognize, become acquainted with, and understand) You, the only true and real God, and [likewise] to know Him, Jesus [as the] Christ (the Anointed One, the Messiah), Whom You have sent.

JOHN 17:3 AMP

❈

In the past you did not know God. You were slaves to gods that were not real. But now you know the true God. Really, it is God who knows you.

GALATIANS 4:8-9 NCV

❈

This is how we may discern [daily, by experience] that we are coming to know Him [to perceive, recognize, understand, and become better acquainted with Him]: if we keep (bear in mind, observe, practice) His teachings (precepts, commandments).

1 JOHN 2:3 AMP

. . . I will pray.

Precious Lord,

In the past, I've been content with my relationship with You. You were and are still a big God who created heaven and earth and all of its inhabitants, even me. I've always viewed You and even prayed to You from a distance—as if You were so majestic that surely You were unapproachable to hear my petty cries for help. I realize now that I was wrong in my view of You. You are an approachable God who is interested in everything that concerns me.

Lately, I've become thirsty for more of You, Your presence, and Your Word. I desire a deeper and more intimate relationship with You, really knowing You rather than just knowing about You. Share Your heart with me and draw me close enough to hear You whisper my name, opening to me the mystery of Your will and Your answers to my prayers.

I come before You now, asking You to fill me to overflowing with Your presence. I give You my hand and ask You to walk with me each day as my Companion and my Friend. Meet me in the secret place of my heart where I long to sit with You each day.

Amen.

❖

Oh, the fullness, pleasure, sheer excitement
of knowing God on Earth!

Jim Elliot

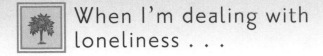

When I'm dealing with loneliness . . .

I am continually with You;
You have taken hold of my right hand.
PSALM 73:23 NASB

❖

[Jesus said] I am with you always, to the close of the age.
MATTHEW 28:20 RSV

❖

[Jesus said] I no longer call you servants,
because a servant does not know what his master is doing.
But I call you friends, because I have made known to you
everything I heard from my Father.
JOHN 15:15 NCV

❖

I meditate on You in the night watches. . . .
My soul follows close behind You;
Your right hand upholds me.
PSALM 63:6,8 NKJV

. . . I will pray.

Heavenly Father,

I looked in the mirror this morning and realized how lonely I feel. I have friends, but even in a room filled with people, I sometimes feel all alone. Have I built my own walls out of fear of getting hurt? If I have, please show me how to let the walls fall and allow others into my life.

I once heard an old saying: If you want to have a friend, you must first learn to be a friend. Father, I know You created me for sharing my heart and life with others. I realize that friendships are precious gifts that need nurturing. Help me be the one who reaches out rather than always waiting for someone to reach out to me. Help me to be the nurturer without worrying if my efforts will be repaid.

I also ask that I would begin to understand the role that comfort and companionship—even friendship—play in my relationship with You. How could I possibly be lonely if I stopped to remember that You are always with me? Push out the loneliness, Lord, and bring in Your love.

Amen.

❋

In every man there is a loneliness, an inner chamber of peculiar life into which God only can enter.

George MacDonald

When I've suffered a loss . . .

God of all healing counsel! He comes alongside us
when we go through hard times, and before you know it,
he brings us alongside someone else who is going through hard
times so that we can be there for that person just as
God was there for us.
2 CORINTHIANS 1:3-4 MSG

❊

This is my comfort in my affliction,
That Your word has revived me. . . .
I have remembered Your ordinances from of old, O LORD,
And comfort myself.
PSALM 119:50,52 NASB

❊

Be gracious to me, O LORD, for I am in distress;
My eye is wasted away from grief. . . .
But as for me, I trust in You, O LORD,
I say, "You are my God."
My times are in Your hand.
PSALM 31:9,14-15 NASB

❊

If your heart is broken, you'll find GOD right there;
if you're kicked in the gut, he'll help you catch your breath.
PSALM 34:18 MSG

. . . I will pray.

Dear God of Comfort,

I'm sitting on the ash heap of my loss, wondering why this had to happen. Everything was going so well. I believe my life is in Your hands and that nothing touches me that has not first passed through You. I know You do not cause the losses in life, but You do allow them, just as You allowed Job to be tested by his trials and all that he lost.

I may never understand why You allowed this in my life, but I want to believe that You have a higher purpose than I can see from where I am sitting. My mother used to say to me as a child, "There's no sense in crying over spilled milk." When something is lost it is lost, and crying doesn't bring it back. Those words didn't necessarily stop my tears from flowing then, and they don't stop my grown-up tears from flowing now. Loss hurts.

Help me come to terms with this loss and comfort me with the peace that passes my understanding. Give me the strength to face tomorrow with hope in You and in the future.

Amen.

❉

On the wings of time grief flies away.

Jean de La Fontaine

When my marriage is in trouble . . .

*Better to live alone in a tumbledown shack
than share a mansion with a nagging spouse.*
PROVERBS 25:24 MSG

❖

*Let the husband render to his wife the affection due her,
and likewise also the wife to her husband.*
1 CORINTHIANS 7:3 NKJV

❖

*They shall be My people, and I will be their God; then I
will give them one heart and one way, that they may fear Me
forever, for the good of them and their children after them.*
JEREMIAH 32:38-39 NKJV

❖

*Submit to one another out of reverence for Christ. Wives,
submit to your husbands as to the Lord. For the husband is
the head of the wife as Christ is the head of the church, his
body, of which he is the Savior. Now as the church submits to
Christ, so also wives should submit to their husbands in
everything. Husbands, love your wives, just as Christ loved
the church and gave himself up for her.*
EPHESIANS 5:21-25

. . . I will pray.

Dear God,

I realize that perfect marriages don't exist. I've learned to deal with the imperfections, but there are times I wonder if my marriage will survive the challenges that we face. If marriage is a holy covenant, why is it so hard to keep the sacredness of love from being wounded and becoming doubtful?

Help me to remember when we first met—the wonderful attributes that first drew me to my mate. Help me see past the problems of everyday living and remember why we made the choice of sharing our lives together. Your Word is clear about the covenant of marriage. Help me do my part to honor and keep my vows. Make me willing to let go of the petty things that mean nothing compared to the greater blessings we share in our relationship. Teach me to trust through the hard places, love through the moments of disagreement, and believe through my tears that there is a strong foundation of commitment that will help us weather this and any future storms that come our way.

Amen.

❊

A good marriage is not one where perfection reigns:
it is a relationship where a healthy perspective
overlooks a multitude of "unresolvables."

James C. Dobson

When I'm searching for meaning . . .

There's nothing better than being wise,
Knowing how to interpret the meaning of life.
ECCLESIASTES 8:1 MSG

❖

He determined the times set for them and
the exact places where they should live.
ACTS 17:26

❖

We know that in everything God works for good with those
who love him, who are called according to his purpose.
ROMANS 8:28 RSV

❖

Be strong and steady, always abounding in the Lord's work,
for you know that nothing you do for the Lord is ever wasted.
1 CORINTHIANS 15:58 TLB

❖

I concentrated with all my might, studying and exploring and
seeking wisdom—the meaning of life.
ECCLESIASTES 7:25 MSG

. . . I will pray.

Dear Heavenly Father,

This morning when I listened to the news on television, I felt an overwhelming sense of sadness over the terrible things that are going on in the world: people left homeless from devastating storms, soldiers enduring unbelievable wartime conditions, and children without enough food to eat.

The more I watched and listened, the more deeply aware I became of my petty complaints. Father, please help me to never take the meaning of life and Your everyday blessings for granted. Awaken me each morning with a thankful heart that remembers what is truly important and precious in life.

Help me to find my deepest sense of purpose through my relationship with You and with others. Teach me gratefulness for the everyday blessings in my life—like clean water to drink, food for my family's table, a comfortable bed to sleep in each night, but most of all, for the blessings of my family and friends. Thank You for showing me that the best things in life are not things.

Amen.

❖

Life can never be wholly dark or wholly futile
once the key to its meaning is in our hands.

J. B. Phillips

When I need a miracle . . .

You are great, and do great miracles. You alone are God.
PSALM 86:10 TLB

❄

You are the God of miracles and wonders!
You still demonstrate your awesome power.
PSALM 77:14 TLB

❄

LORD God of Israel, we praise you.
Only you can work miracles.
PSALM 72:18 CEV

❄

How we thank you, Lord!
Your mighty miracles give proof that you care.
PSALM 75:1 TLB

❄

Everyone shall stand in awe and confess the greatness
of the miracles of God; at last they will realize
what amazing things he does.
PSALM 64:9 TLB

. . . I will pray.

Dear Heavenly Father,

I know that many people do not believe in miracles. Miracles are seemingly scarce in this day and age, at least to man's natural, intellectual, and grown-up mind and eye. But, Father, if I read Your Word correctly, it says that You have not changed. It says that You are the same today as yesterday and that You will be the same forever.

I'm standing on that promise today, Father. I'm believing that if You once worked miracles, You are still a miracle-working God, able to do far more than anything my finite mind can think or comprehend. You can still open blind eyes, make the lame walk, and cause the deaf to hear. You heal, set events in motion, and change and rearrange situations. I know You are able and willing to create a miracle of any proportion.

I cannot imagine how You will intervene, but I believe in You and realize that only You can change the circumstances that are affecting my life. I need a miracle, God, and I'm asking You for enough childlike faith to simply believe that all things are possible.

Amen.

�֍

A miracle is an event beyond the power of any known physical law to produce; it is a spiritual occurrence produced by the power of God, a marvel, a wonder.

Billy Graham

When I'm struggling with my past . . .

Forget the former things; do not dwell on the past.
See, I am doing a new thing! Now it springs up;
do you not perceive it? I am making a way in the desert
and streams in the wasteland.

ISAIAH 43:18-19

✤

You were taught, with regard to your former way of life,
to put off your old self, which is being corrupted by its
deceitful desires; to be made new in the attitude of your
minds; and to put on the new self, created to be like God in
true righteousness and holiness.

EPHESIANS 4:22-24

✤

Surely you know that the people who do wrong will not
inherit God's kingdom. . . . In the past, some of you were like
that, but you were washed clean. You were made holy, and
you were made right with God in the name of the Lord Jesus
Christ and in the Spirit of our God.

1 CORINTHIANS 6:9,11 NCV

. . . I will pray.

Lord Jesus,

Just when I think I've really gotten past the bad parts of my former life, I find myself acting the same old way, as if I'm in a time warp. Even my vocabulary reverts. To hear me, a person would never think I'm a "new creation in Christ." I wonder myself.

That's what happened today, so here I am, talking with You about it. You are my Savior. I have put my complete trust in You. I have seen positive changes in my attitudes—some that occurred overnight and some that developed over time. You have helped me to forgive the people who did me the most harm when I was young. You have provided me with new friends and practical wisdom for life.

You don't seem to have given up on me, no matter how many times I get embroiled in old patterns.

Maybe I need a kind of spiritual "workout." To get past my current events, I need to exercise my faith muscles a little, to actively put my faith in Your goodness. I need to purposely remember the encouraging developments and press past these setbacks. Only by the power of Your Spirit can I keep on keeping on. Hang on to me, Lord.

Amen.

❊

In Christ we can move out of our past
into a meaningful present and a breathtaking future.
Erwin W. Lutzer

When I need patience . . .

We also pray that you will be strengthened
with his glorious power so that you will have all the
patience and endurance you need.

COLOSSIANS 1:11 NLT

❧

We continue to shout our praise even when we're hemmed in
with troubles, because we know how troubles can develop
passionate patience in us, and how that patience in turn
forges the tempered steel of virtue, keeping us alert
for whatever God will do next.

ROMANS 5:3-4 MSG

❧

See how the farmer waits for the precious fruit of the earth,
waiting patiently for it until it receives the early and latter
rain. You also be patient.

JAMES 5:7-8 NKJV

❧

We have proved ourselves to be what we claim by our
wholesome lives and by our understanding of the Gospel
and by our patience.

2 CORINTHIANS 6:6 TLB

. . . I will pray.

Dear Lord,

The picture in my children's Bible shows You as a shepherd. It reminds me of how shepherds have to be supremely patient as they tend their flocks. I can't imagine one impatiently tapping his foot and checking his watch while his animals mosey along.

Patience is part of Your makeup, and I believe You want it to be part of mine. Maybe that's why You allow my lack of patience to be exposed by my circumstances.

I'd like to be able to say, "It's just the way I am. It's part of my personality to be quick, aggressive, and sure of myself." But this isn't the first time I've found myself in a situation that requires me to wait patiently—and each time the waiting gets tougher. Still, I've learned this much: my impatience serves no productive purpose at all.

It's a good thing You don't have a limit on the number of times I can come to You for this. Forgive me for being such a slow learner. I sure am glad for Your patience with me. Thank You in advance for Your help.

Amen.

❧

Patience is bitter, but its fruit is sweet.

Jean Jacques Rousseau

When I need peace . . .

Happy are those who find wisdom,
and those who get understanding. . . .
Her ways are ways of pleasantness,
and all her paths are peace.
PROVERBS 3:13,17 NRSV

❊

I will listen to what God the LORD will say;
he promises peace to his people, his saints.
PSALM 85:8

❊

To all of you that are in Christ Jesus (the Messiah), may there be peace (every kind of peace and blessing, especially peace with God, and freedom from fears, agitating passions, and moral conflicts).
1 PETER 5:14 AMP

❊

Embrace peace—don't let it get away!
PSALM 34:14 MSG

. . . I will pray.

Dear Lord,

You are called the Prince of Peace. Does that mean You can take me into a place that is peace-filled—even while I continue to dwell here, where the decibel level is high, and worse, the stress and anxiety levels threaten to make "peace" a quaint concept?

In my search for peace, I don't want to resort to second-best tactics to escape the agitation that is boiling in my heart and mind. Reading a good book by the fireside might provide some relief, but I suspect it will be temporary. Even cloistered contemplatives can become restless and impatient.

So my prayer is this: keep me in the center of Your will. Help me to keep my heart pure and my feet on Your path. Show me how to backtrack to the place where I lost my peace this time. I realize it may prove to be the same place I lose it over and over. Please provide me with the insight that I need, the practical action steps, and the ability to follow You out of the commotion around me and inside me.

Thank You, Lord, for making me a full citizen of Your kingdom of peace.

Amen

✤

All His glory and beauty come from within,
and there He delights to dwell, His visits there are frequent, His conversations sweet, His comforts refreshing, and His peace passing all understanding.

Thomas à Kempis

When I'm suffering
persecution . . .

Who shall separate us from the love of Christ?
Shall trouble or hardship or persecution or famine or
nakedness or danger or sword?
ROMANS 8:35

❊

[Jesus said] Remember the word that I said to you,
"A servant is not greater than his master." If they persecuted
me, they will persecute you.
JOHN 15:20 RSV

❊

[Jesus said] Love your enemies, bless them that curse you,
do good to them that hate you, and pray for them which
despitefully use you, and persecute you.
MATTHEW 5:44 KJV

❊

[Jesus said] You're blessed when your commitment to
God provokes persecution. The persecution drives you
even deeper into God's kingdom.
MATTHEW 5:10 MSG

. . . I will pray.

Almighty God,

The word "persecution" doesn't have to apply only to Christians long ago or far away, does it? I can't think of a better word to describe what's happening to me right now. People are believing lying accusations about me. I do seem to be suffering persecution, discrimination, and exclusion.

I don't want to become paranoid. At the same time, I don't want to assume I'm right about this. What if it turns out that I deserve this kind of backbiting?

Whether I deserve it or not, this is a miserable situation. I'm forced to my knees before You. Here it is—all of it. I lay it before You—the details, my reactions, and my certainty that You are in charge.

From this position, I can see better. I see that my first step, whether or not this is fair, is to accept trial—maybe even thank You for it. Persecution puts me in pretty good company.

Whatever happens, nothing can separate me from Your loving care. Fortify my spirit. Please furnish the wisdom I need. Show me what to do after this prayer, if anything. Thank You for keeping me dependent upon You.

Amen.

❖

The servant of Christ must never be surprised
if he has to drink of the same cup with his Lord.

J. C. Ryle

When I need protection . . .

[God] orders his angels to protect you wherever you go.
PSALM 91:11 TLB

❧

You protect me with salvation-armor;
you hold me up with a firm hand,
caress me with your gentle ways.
PSALM 18:35 MSG

❧

The LORD is my light and the one who saves me.
I fear no one.
The LORD protects my life;
I am afraid of no one.
PSALM 27:1 NCV

❧

Deliver me from my enemies, O my God,
protect me from those who rise up against me.
PSALM 59:1 RSV

. . . I will pray.

Mighty Lord,

I need Your protection—at home, at work, everywhere. Each time I step outside my door, get into my car, stop off at the mall, walk across the street, I'm in danger. There simply is no safe place for me and my loved ones outside the circle of Your watchful care. We depend on Your strong shield around us.

Teach us, Lord, to live responsibly—though not fearfully—in a dangerous world. It's a privilege to put my faith and trust in Your faithful care. The Bible says that You've even charged Your angels to watch out for us.

I'm grateful that You protect us spiritually as well. I know that war is being waged in the heavens—a war for my soul and the souls of those You have chosen to live in intimate relationship with You. Keep us always aware, always watchful, and always confident that we are safe and secure as long as we walk in Your ways.

This world is a treacherous place, Lord—You know that even better than I. But You've given me the armor I need to live safely here and fulfill Your will for my life. I thank You for that.

Amen.

The center of God's will is our only safety.

Betsie ten Boom

When I'm feeling
sadness . . .

Be kind to me, GOD. . . .
I've cried my eyes out; I feel hollow inside. . . .
Warm me, your servant, with a smile;
save me because you love me.
PSALM 31:9-10 MSG

❖

You changed my sorrow into dancing.
You took away my clothes of sadness,
and clothed me in happiness.
PSALM 30:11 NCV

❖

The ransomed of the LORD will return.
They will enter Zion with singing;
everlasting joy will crown their heads.
Gladness and joy will overtake them,
and sorrow and sighing will flee away.
ISAIAH 35:10

❖

Blessed be the Lord, Who bears our burdens and carries us
day by day, even the God Who is our salvation! Selah
[pause, and calmly think of that]!
PSALM 68:19 AMP

. . . I will pray.

Precious Lord,

It's just been blow after blow lately, and I'm feeling pretty beaten down. I dread the next piece of bad news. Every day there's been something. The sadness keeps me awake at night and the fatigue keeps me sad.

Instead of just muddling through this low period, I'd rather ask for Your help. I don't want to resort to a mere crutch to cheer myself up. I know that would be such a flimsy, temporary fix. Besides, I just remembered that the Bible calls You the God of all comfort. I'm going to camp there for a while, if You'll let me. I'm counting on Your being the God of all comfort for me now. I believe You have promised to help me when I feel so low.

Like a child, I'm asking for what I need, which is comfort and encouragement. I don't expect to be happy-go-lucky—just delivered from my tears and sadness. Let me feel Your strong heartbeat as I lean hard against You. Match my feeble heartbeats to Your strong ones. You aren't weary or sad. You are God.

Amen.

❋

No one needs to be downcast, for Jesus is the joy of heaven, and it is His joy to enter into sorrowful hearts.

Frederick William Faber

When I can't sleep . . .

I will both lie down in peace, and sleep;
For You alone, O LORD, make me dwell in safety.
PSALM 4:8 NKJV

❧

If you sit down, you will not be afraid;
when you lie down, your sleep will be sweet.
PROVERBS 3:24 RSV

❧

The Lord gives sleep to those he loves.
PSALM 127:2 NCV

❧

The fear of the LORD leads to life,
So that one may sleep satisfied, untouched by evil.
PROVERBS 19:23 NASB

❧

Find rest, O my soul, in God alone; my hope comes from him.
PSALM 62:5

. . . I will pray.

Dear Lord,

I'm tired, and I want so much to be able to simply fall asleep. I don't want to use this time to pray, except to pray myself to sleep, noble as it might seem to be to pray during the so-called watches of the night. I become more wakeful when I start thinking about what I should pray for. I'll leave the watches of the night to Your faithful care.

They say that troubles become magnified in the night. Surely they do. My mind is busy inventing new troubles to keep the old ones company. Meantime, the rest of the household sleeps as if it hadn't a care in the world.

Should I just get up? Have I been sleeping a little, even while I think I'm lying here awake? How am I going to stay awake at work tomorrow? The clock says three o'clock. Is it possible that I've been awake this whole time?

Who is keeping watch at this hour? Oh, of course—You are. Maybe just being in Your presence will allow me to relax—and find peace and rest. Either way, I'll be safe and comfortable right here with You. Good night, Lord.

Amen.

❋

Tired nature's sweet restorer, balmy sleep!

Edward Young

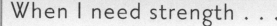

When I need strength . . .

Incline Your ear to me, rescue me quickly;
Be to me a rock of strength,
A stronghold to save me.
PSALM 31:2 NASB

❋

Those who wait on the LORD
Shall renew their strength;
They shall mount up with wings like eagles,
They shall run and not be weary,
They shall walk and not faint.
ISAIAH 40:31 NKJV

❋

I will boast . . . about my weaknesses, so that Christ's power
may rest on me. . . . For when I am weak, then I am strong.
2 CORINTHIANS 12:9-10

❋

The rock of my strength, my refuge is in God.
PSALM 62:7 NASB

. . . I will pray.

Lord my God,

Here I am again, driven by my weakness to the security of Your promise to strengthen and sustain me. Holding tight to Your promises, I find myself relaxing already, resting in Your presence. My tension headache is disappearing, I can think clearly, and all the anxiety is seeping away.

Lord, when will I learn to come to You before the crisis rages inside me, before my own strength is entirely spent, before I can do little more than stagger into Your arms? I want to correct that last-moment, last-resort approach. This time, I'm going to take Your promises with me when I leave this time of prayer. I will call on them at the beginning and end of each new day until they become part of my inner person.

Thank You, Lord, for always being there for me, for lifting me up when I'm down, for replacing my weakness with Your strength. I've always been afraid to admit my weakness, but I see now that my shortcoming is my opportunity to experience Your overflowing abundance. Thank You for being my Rock.

Amen.

❋

When a man has no strength, if he leans on God,
he becomes powerful.

Dwight Lyman Moody

When I'm facing
temptation . . .

Blessed is anyone who endures temptation. Such a one has
stood the test and will receive the crown of life that the Lord
has promised to those who love him.
JAMES 1:12 NRSV

❖

[Jesus said] Keep watching and praying that you
may not enter into temptation; the spirit is willing,
but the flesh is weak.
MATTHEW 26:41 NASB

❖

No temptation has overtaken you except such as is common
to man; but God is faithful, who will not allow you to be
tempted beyond what you are able, but with the
temptation will also make the way of escape,
that you may be able to bear it.
1 CORINTHIANS 10:13 NKJV

❖

The devil, your enemy, goes around like a roaring lion
looking for someone to eat. Refuse to give in to him, by
standing strong in your faith.
1 PETER 5:8-9 NCV

. . . I will pray.

Blessed Lord,

I have heard the following quote attributed to Martin Luther: "You can't stop the birds from flying over your head, but you don't have to let them build a nest in your hair," which means that everyone is tempted, but we can choose not to yield.

But I have discovered something: merely understanding that statement is no guarantee that the birds will simply continue to circle the airport without coming in for a landing.

Today, I'm still shaking some of yesterday's nesting material out of my coiffure. Now I'm more certain than ever that I need to stay close to You, talk to You, listen to what You say. If we're close, I can heed Your voice more easily, and it won't get lost in the noise of the "birds." You can keep me in motion, so that no bird will ever consider me a suitable nesting place. If we're close, You can even chase some of them away. I don't have eyes in the back of my head. Keep an eye out for me, Lord. My prayer is simple: I want to be close to You.

Amen.

❋

The whole effort—the object—of temptation is to induce us to substitute something else for God. To obscure God.

R. H. Stewart

When I'm experiencing trials . . .

Count it all joy when you fall into various trials,
knowing that the testing of your faith produces patience.
But let patience have its perfect work, that you may be perfect
and complete, lacking nothing.
JAMES 1:2-4 NKJV

❈

Beloved, do not think it strange concerning the fiery trial
which is to try you, as though some strange thing happened to
you; but rejoice to the extent that you partake of Christ's
sufferings, that when His glory is revealed,
you may also be glad with exceeding joy.
1 PETER 4:12-13 NKJV

❈

[The Lord] reached down from heaven and took me
and drew me out of my great trials. He rescued me
from deep waters.
PSALM 18:16 TLB

❈

Endure trials for the sake of discipline.
God is treating you as children; for what child is there whom
a parent does not discipline?
HEBREWS 12:7 NRSV

. . . I will pray.

Dear Lord,

You are my advocate. You are the One who always pleads my cause—and, Lord, I know that You never lose. I just need some reassurance for this failing human heart of mine. This trial is one of the most difficult I've ever experienced, and I need to feel Your presence here with me. I need the total assurance that You are right here by my side.

I'm asking for relief, but not exemption. I want You to resolve my troubles as quickly as possible without sacrificing their value to the betterment of my character. Assuming You want me to learn something from this trial, please make the lesson as clear as possible. I certainly don't relish the idea of going through all of this twice!

I need persevering faith to keep applying to You for strength and wisdom and peace. And my spirit needs a lift. Show me where the joy is to be found in this dark time.

My hope and my confidence are in You. You won't let me settle for a Pollyanna-ish silver lining when there is a gold mine to be plumbed. Thank You for being my Strength and my Comfort.

Amen.

❧

In this life we will encounter hurts and trials that we will not be able to change; we are just going to have to allow them to change us.

Ron Lee Davis

When I need wisdom . . .

Behold, You desire truth in the innermost being,
And in the hidden part You will make me know wisdom.
PSALM 51:6 NASB

❋

If any of you is lacking in wisdom, ask God, who gives to all
generously and ungrudgingly, and it will be given you.
JAMES 1:5 NRSV

❋

Happy is the person who finds wisdom,
the one who gets understanding.
Wisdom is worth more than silver;
it brings more profit than gold.
Wisdom is more precious than rubies;
nothing you could want is equal to it.
With her right hand wisdom offers you a long life,
and with her left hand she gives you riches and honor.
PROVERBS 3:13-16 NCV

❋

I will bless the LORD who guides me;
even at night my heart instructs me.
I know the LORD is always with me.
I will not be shaken, for he is right beside me.
PSALM 16:7-8 NLT

. . . I will pray.

Dear Lord,

By Your grace, I know I can receive a measure of Your wisdom right now. I need it today, right here, right now, so that I can unravel this complicated mess. The human, emotional element is making it even worse, but I know You can help me make sense of it all.

You encourage us to ask for Your wisdom, so that's what I'm doing. By whatever means, put Your solutions at my disposal. Speak my language, dear Lord—make this thing fathomable for me. I'm asking and expecting that You will respond. I need to know how to handle this situation in a way that is productive and life-giving to everyone involved. Where do I begin, Lord?

The Bible says that Your wisdom is there for me whenever I ask. And You know, Lord, that I've asked before at other times of need. You've never failed me. Each time I found my thoughts turning like the tumblers of a padlock. Before long, I had the right combination and we were moving toward a solution.

Do it again! Dispose of my flawed reasoning and infuse me with Your wisdom and counsel.

Amen.

❖

Knowledge comes, but wisdom lingers.
Alfred Lord Tennyson

When I have concerns at work . . .

Do your work with enthusiasm. Work as if you were serving the Lord, not as if you were serving only men and women.
EPHESIANS 6:7 NCV

❋

My life is worth nothing unless I use it for doing the work assigned me by the Lord Jesus.
ACTS 20:24 NLT

❋

In all the work you are doing, work the best you can. Work as if you were doing it for the Lord, not for people. Remember that you will receive your reward from the Lord, which he promised to his people. You are serving the Lord Christ.
COLOSSIANS 3:23-24 NCV

❋

To enjoy your work and to accept your lot in life— that is indeed a gift from God. The person who does that will not need to look back with sorrow on his past, for God gives him joy.
ECCLESIASTES 5:19-20 TLB

. . . I will pray.

My Father,

The Bible says that work is a gift from You, but I don't see how. Sometimes I feel as if I've been captured by aliens and I'm just trying to survive until the rescue ship arrives so I can finally lock my office door and flee.

All the backbiting and infighting and politics and injustice and one-upmanship: Everyone plays the blame game, and nobody seems to want to take responsibility for mistakes. And here's the worst part—way too often I find myself caught up in it all. One minute I'm getting things done, and then I run into someone in the hall who throws some juicy little tidbit out there. Or I get asked a question in a meeting—the simplest thing, really—and suddenly I'm all entangled. Makes me wonder if my coworkers, who are all pretty nice people on their own, aren't just caught up in it too.

Lord, help me to do more than hide in my office. Give me the courage to take a strong stand for kindness and sanity. And show me how to do it without being judgmental or condescending. I want my job to be what it was intended to be—Your delightful gift.

Amen.

✻

O Lord, renew our spirits and draw our hearts
unto Yourself, that our work may not be
as a burden but a delight.

Benjamin Jenks

God, be merciful to me;
On Thy grace I rest my plea;
In Thy vast, abounding grace,
My transgressions all erase.
Wash me wholly from my sin;
Cleanse from every ill within.

The Psalter

Prayers of
Confession

Lifting My Voice to God
When I Need Forgiveness

When I've made foolish choices . . .

He shows how to distinguish right from wrong,
how to find the right decision every time.
PROVERBS 2:9 TLB

✤

Who are they that fear the LORD*?*
He will teach them the way that they should choose.
PSALM 25:12 NRSV

✤

Where there is no counsel, the people fall;
But in the multitude of counselors there is safety.
PROVERBS 11:14 NKJV

✤

Without counsel, plans go awry,
But in the multitude of counselors they are established.
PROVERBS 15:22 NKJV

✤

The Spirit gives us desires that are opposite from what the sinful nature desires. . . . And your choices are never free from this conflict.
GALATIANS 5:17 NLT

. . . I will pray.

Dear Lord,

The "what ifs" are overwhelming me now. I know it was my own choice, and I have to lie in the bed I made. Because I was convinced that it was too good an opportunity to pass up, I made a decision that affects my whole family. I refused to listen to objections. Now we know it was a mistake, and we're stuck. And it's all my fault.

I should have listened. Friends, family, coworkers—they were right. Even if all of them had been wrong, I should have at least listened better.

At least I'm willing to admit my foolishness. But that's not a lot of practical help.

I guess now I have to make the best of it—with Your patient help. You haven't shut me off from Your help just because I made such a bad decision. You have lots of children who make bad choices. You redeem every one, if You are asked to.

Forgive me for ignoring the advice You were trying to convey to me. What it amounts to is arrogance. Forgive me, Lord.

I want my heart's desire to become the same as Yours.

Amen.

❋

By the mercy of God we may repent a wrong choice and alter the consequences by making a new and right choice.

A. W. Tozer

When I've become critical and judgmental . . .

[Jesus said] Don't pick on people, jump on their failures, criticize their faults—unless, of course, you want the same treatment. That critical spirit has a way of boomeranging.
MATTHEW 7:1-2 MSG

❊

The whole Law can be summed up in this one command: "Love others as you love yourself." But if instead of showing love among yourselves you are always critical and catty, watch out! Beware of ruining each other.
GALATIANS 5:14-15 TLB

❊

Don't speak evil against each other. . . . If you criticize each other and condemn each other, then you are criticizing and condemning God's law. . . . God alone, who made the law, can rightly judge among us. . . . So what right do you have to condemn your neighbor?
JAMES 4:11-12 NLT

❊

Don't grumble about each other, my brothers and sisters, or God will judge you.
JAMES 5:9 NLT

. . . I will pray.

Dear Lord,

I'll admit it right up front: You are the only true Judge. I'm not.

And although You judge strictly, You judge fairly—and You judge with a heart that's filled with all the love in the universe.

It's a slippery slope, for sure. Taking one step, uttering one word of criticism, seems to start a small avalanche of judgmentalism in my heart. Soon, I begin to reap what I've sown.

Asking for Your forgiveness is the place to start. (How many times now have I done that?) And yet, this time, I'd also like to apply for a loan, a portion of Your patient love. I need Your love to help me see in a new light that guy I just described as a "bonehead." Surely that is not what You would call him! Help me see his needs through Your eyes. Enable me to encourage him instead of tearing him down, even if that happens only in my thoughts.

Before I can truly reform, I need a permanent supply of Your love in my heart, along with a very strong reminder that I am not God myself. I trust that this is a prayer You will answer almost before I've finished praying it.

Amen.

❁

The faults of others are like headlights of
an approaching car—they always seem more
glaring than our own.
Author Unknown

When I've failed to keep my word . . .

[The Lord commanded] If a man makes a promise to the
LORD or says he will do something special, he must keep his
promise. He must do what he said.

NUMBERS 30:2 NCV

✤

If you do not make the promise, you will not be guilty.
You must do whatever you say you will do, because you chose
to make the promise to the LORD your God.

DEUTERONOMY 23:22-23 NCV

✤

Keep your word even when it costs you.

PSALM 15:4 MSG

✤

O God, . . . help me never to tell a lie.

PROVERBS 30:7-8 TLB

✤

I know, my God, that you test the heart and
are pleased with integrity.

1 CHRONICLES 29:17

. . . I will pray.

Faithful Lord,

I'm here to own up to something I shouldn't have done. Just now, my neighbor called to find out why I didn't do what I said I'd do for him. The real reason is that I forgot. I didn't look at my calendar. I just plain forgot.

You would think I could have said so. But no, not only did I fail to follow through on my original promise, I also failed to be honest. I told him I had a family emergency. That's a lie, and not even a white one. The truth is, I failed to keep my word and then I told a lie so I would look better.

I could have told the truth: "I'm so sorry. I completely forgot. I must find a better way to remember. Please forgive me."

Now I have a choice. I can either feel like a worm whenever I see my neighbor, or I can, well, feel like a worm and tell him the truth.

When You said we'd be "fishers of men," I didn't realize that sometimes we would have to play the worm to Your hook. I pray that my humiliating honesty will keep him as my friend and perhaps help me become more responsible.

Amen.

He who is slow in making a promise is most likely to be faithful in the performance of it.

Jean Jacques Rousseau

When I've been hurtful to others . . .

*The tongue runs wild, a wanton killer. With our tongues
we bless God our Father; with the same tongues we curse
the very men and women he made in his image.
Curses and blessings out of the same mouth! My friends,
this can't go on. A spring doesn't gush fresh water one day
and brackish the next, does it?*

JAMES 3:8-11 MSG

❖

*[Jesus said] When you are offering your gift at the altar,
if you remember that your brother or sister has something
against you, leave your gift there before the altar and go;
first be reconciled to your brother or sister,
and then come and offer your gift.*

MATTHEW 5:23-24 NRSV

❖

*Put these things out of your life: anger, bad temper, doing
or saying things to hurt others, and using evil words when
you talk. Do not lie to each other. You have left your old
sinful life and the things you did before. You have begun to
live the new life, in which you are being made new and are
becoming like the One who made you.*

COLOSSIANS 3:8-10 NCV

. . . I will pray.

Dear Father,

Once again, I see that I have hurt someone unnecessarily. In my headlong rush to be first and best, I trampled her spirit. We were just having a conversation; it didn't have to turn into a clash. She cringed visibly when I spoke that last sentence so hastily, the one about "losers."

Now what?

Should I eat humble pie and go back to her, or would that only stir up the hurtfulness all over again? (Maybe she's forgotten about it already.) In my defense, I should say that I was only giving her a taste of her own medicine. But I'm pretty sure that my conscience wouldn't be smarting so much if it were okay to do that, so here I am asking You to forgive me.

And yes, I'll call her and apologize. Maybe we can start loving each other better. To replace our pattern of hurting each other, we are going to need Your grace.

One good thing comes from this at least—this sort of thing keeps me ever so aware of my need for Your grace. Where would I be without You?

Amen.

�֎

Cold words freeze people, and hot words scorch them, and bitter words make them bitter, and wrathful words make them wrathful. Kind words . . . soothe, and quiet, and comfort the hearer.

Blaise Pascal

When I've stooped to lies and deception . . .

Keep deception and lies far from me.
PROVERBS 30:8 NASB

❖

*Listen to me! For I have important information for you.
Everything I say is right and true, for I hate lies and
every kind of deception.*
PROVERBS 8:6-7 TLB

❖

*He who speaks the truth gives honest evidence,
but a false witness utters deceit.*
PROVERBS 12:17 RSV

❖

*Putting away falsehood, let every one speak the truth with his
neighbor, for we are members one of another.*
EPHESIANS 4:25 RSV

❖

*[Jesus said] He [the devil] is a liar and the father of lies.
But . . . I tell the truth.*
JOHN 8:44-45 NRSV

. . . I will pray.

O Lord,

I didn't want to get the blame for the careless, selfish stunt I pulled, so I lied about it. I was shocked to think that I could do such a thing, but I'm pretty sure You weren't. After all, You see my heart. You know what I'm really capable of—much better even than I do.

So . . . now that I've come clean, Lord, I need to know what to do next. For starters, I plan to apologize for my bad behavior and my silly lie. But confession is—I'm sure—barely more than the price of admission. I also need to know what character flaw allowed me to do such a thing in the first place, and I need to know how to keep it from happening again.

I'm sure it won't be easy to face my own flaw, but I'm ready, Lord. Drag it out in front of me and let me renounce it. If I try to cut and run, hem me in until I deal with it. I know that being deceitful is not honoring You. It hurts me to know that I've treated You with disrespect. I want to do better. Thank You, Lord, for the joy of being free to choose truth.

Amen.

❉

The essence of lying is in deception, not in words;
a lie may be told by silence, by equivocation,
by the accent on a syllable, by a glance of the eye
attaching a peculiar significance to a sentence.

John Ruskin

When I've been prideful and arrogant . . .

"*Talk no more so very proudly,*
let not arrogance come from your mouth."
1 SAMUEL 2:3 NRSV

❖

When pride comes, then comes disgrace;
but with the humble is wisdom.
PROVERBS 11:2 RSV

❖

Pride goes before destruction and haughtiness before a fall.
PROVERBS 16:18 TLB

❖

Pride will ruin people,
but those who are humble will be honored.
PROVERBS 29:23 NCV

❖

Love is . . . not arrogant or rude.
1 CORINTHIANS 13:4-5 RSV

. . . I will pray.

Heavenly Father,

I'm on that oh-so-familiar fence again. This time, for a change, I'd like to get off on Your side of it. It's the fence of my own self-seeking arrogance. Even when I recognize the way my self-importance has once again sullied a conversation, I sit tight on this fence-top, only halfway dismayed. The other half of me is, well, just too proud to want to let go of the flimsily constructed image I have projected. I like having people think I'm special.

But I am gradually growing to deplore the whole thing. I've noticed that it makes me much less trustful and peaceful inside. I don't care much about other people. Worst of all, You seem far away when I am on this fence.

You've given me nudges and hints that I need to surrender my pride to You. I have taken them too lightly. I'm sorry, Lord. This is major. It affects everything. You are the Lord of my life. If You want to address my pride, You can do that. I don't want to ruin my spiritual journey with You by being on one long ego trip.

Amen.

✷

Pride is the ground in which all the other sins grow,
and the parent from which all the other sins come.

William Barclay

When I've sinned
(broken God's laws) . . .

[Peter said] Everyone who believes in him receives
forgiveness of sins through his name.
ACTS 10:43 NRSV

⁂

Blessed are those whose iniquities are forgiven,
and whose sins are covered; blessed is the one against whom
the Lord will not reckon sin.
ROMANS 4:7-8 NRSV

⁂

Keep your servant also from willful sins;
may they not rule over me.
Then will I be blameless,
innocent of great transgression.
PSALM 19:13

⁂

If we admit our sins—make a clean breast of them
—he won't let us down; he'll be true to himself.
He'll forgive our sins and purge us of all wrongdoing.
1 JOHN 1:9 MSG

. . . I will pray.

Dear God,

You ought to throw the book at me. For weeks, I've been acting as if You and Your laws didn't matter, especially when I'm surrounded by people who don't believe You are real.

I'm like a chameleon: I blend into any environment. Apparently, rather than being salt and light to the world around me, I'd rather be accepted by it. I know my accommodating behavior comes from my human nature; I only wish diagnosing it could excuse it.

The blunt truth is that my conduct comes under the category of sin, and I need to confess it to You. (I'd prefer to call it a "weakness" or a "flaw," even "wrongdoing" or a "peccadillo"—I like the sound of that one.) But I do know right from wrong. My gossip is sin; my complaining is sin; my evasion of duty is sin. I know there's at least one line in Your Book about each one of those.

If You have to throw the book at me, Lord, please make sure it's the Good Book, and please bookmark some lines about Your forgiveness. Save me from myself.

Amen.

❈

Christ's death on the cross included a sacrifice for all our sins, past, present, and future. Every sin that you will ever commit has already been paid for.

Erwin W. Lutzer

When I've neglected my responsibilities . . .

*Don't try to avoid responsibility by saying you didn't know
about it. For God knows all hearts, and he sees you.*
PROVERBS 24:12 NLT

❊

*[Jesus said] I tell you that on the Judgment Day people
will be responsible for every careless thing they have said.
The words you have said will be used to judge you.
Some of your words will prove you right,
but some of your words will prove you guilty.*
MATTHEW 12:36-37 NCV

❊

*Each person should judge his own actions and not
compare himself with others. Then he can be proud for
what he himself has done. Each person must be
responsible for himself.*
GALATIANS 6:4-5 NCV

❊

*If God has given you leadership ability,
take the responsibility seriously.*
ROMANS 12:8 NLT

. . . I will pray.

Dear Lord Jesus,

Really, there's no excuse. I have the time, the energy, and the intelligence to do what I'm supposed to do. I intend to do everything. I even make lists.

Then "something comes up," or "the day is just crazy," or "it's too late to finish, so why start?" I procrastinate. Mañana. Later, OK? "I'll call you back." "I'll get it done before the weekend." "I'll pick it up soon." "I'll make a point of it."

Hallmark should start a line of "belated" cards designed just for me. It's more than belated birthdays—I have a responsibility problem.

Sometimes I even make fervent promises, but I renege . . . with golden excuses: "I committed myself to too much, and I just couldn't manage all of it." "I had every intention of doing it, but then I switched to a new calendar." "My memory is such a sieve."

Maybe I should get an absentee ballot for life. Maybe Weasel should become my middle name.

Tell me straight—what do You hold me accountable for? Then, Lord, please convert me from being such a shirker. No joke. I know I can't do better on my own. I need Your help. Thank You for Your help.

Amen.

❋

Character—the willingness to accept
responsibility for one's own life—
is the source from which self-respect springs.

Joan Didion

When I need to be in right relationship with God . . .

Cultivate your own relationship with God.
ROMANS 14:22 MSG

❖

*Your fellowship with God enables you to gain
a victory over the Evil One.*
1 JOHN 2:14 MSG

❖

*[Jesus said] Look! I have been standing at the door and
I am constantly knocking. If anyone hears me calling him
and opens the door, I will come in and fellowship
with him and he with me.*
REVELATION 3:20 TLB

❖

*We can rejoice in our wonderful new relationship with
God—all because of what our Lord Jesus Christ has done for
us in making us friends of God.*
ROMANS 5:11 NLT

. . . I will pray.

Heavenly Father,

I declare to You and to anyone anywhere who may be listening: You are my Lord and my God and You are in charge of everything. I want this fact to rule my life. I don't want to wander away from You, even for short intervals. I want my wandering days to be over for good.

Please point out to me anything that may be between us, Lord. I will do whatever You say. I want to bridge the dark void that has separated us. I want only to be with You.

Forgive my arrogance. What was I thinking when I acted as if the world revolved around me? You couldn't occupy the central place in my life when I stationed myself there. There's room for only one of us at a time.

Thank You for Your supreme patience, for the way You so delicately guided me to Your feet. Thank You for relieving me from the burden of being my own savior. What an impossible assignment I had taken on! Rule and reign in me, Father, through the Holy Spirit.

Amen.

✽

Religion is humans trying to work their way to God through good works. Christianity is God coming to men and women through Jesus Christ offering them a relationship with Himself.

Josh McDowell

When I've exacted vengeance . . .

Don't say, "I'll pay you back for the wrong you did."
Wait for the LORD, and he will make things right.
PROVERBS 20:22 NCV

❋

Beloved, never avenge yourselves, but leave room for the
wrath of God; for it is written, "Vengeance is mine, I will
repay, says the Lord." No, "if your enemies are hungry, feed
them; if they are thirsty, give them something to drink; for by
doing this you will heap burning coals on their heads." Do not
be overcome by evil, but overcome evil with good.
ROMANS 12:19-21 NRSV

❋

Do not seek revenge or bear a grudge against one of your
people, but love your neighbor as yourself. I am the LORD.
LEVITICUS 19:18

❋

[Love] is not touchy or fretful or resentful;
it takes no account of the evil done to it
[it pays no attention to a suffered wrong].
1 CORINTHIANS 13:5 AMP

. . . I will pray.

O Lord God,

I am pleading for Your mercy this time. I don't know how to undo the wrong I've done. I did exactly what You've told us we should never do: I took revenge on someone I felt had wronged me. Blinded with rage, I went on a smear campaign of my own, planting insinuations, questioning his credibility, recruiting allies.

If only I had simply surrendered it all to You. You would have taken care of it. You would have soothed me. I know Your justice would have arrived in due time.

I have now found out—the hard way—how it feels to usurp Your job. There was a brief moment of satisfaction when I turned to retaliate, but now I am crushed with guilt. Worst of all, my heart has grown cold. My mind is swamped with imagined scenarios and vituperative words. This is much worse than I felt when I first found myself offended.

Please forgive me, Lord. Wash me clean and give me the courage to do the right thing in this situation. Humble pie is hard to eat, but it makes me all the more grateful for the joy and peace that come with making things right with You.

Amen.

✳

The noblest vengeance is to forgive.

Henry George Bohn

Make me an intercessor,
One who can really pray,
One of "the Lord's remembrancers"
By night as well as day.

Frances Ridley Havergal

Prayers of
Intercession

Lifting My Voice to God
on Behalf of Others

When my child is struggling with addiction . . .

On God rests my deliverance and my honor;
my mighty rock, my refuge is God.
<small>PSALM 62:7 RSV</small>

❖

Behold, the eye of the Lord is on those who fear Him,
On those who hope in His mercy,
To deliver their soul from death,
And to keep them alive in famine.
<small>PSALM 33:18-19 NKJV</small>

❖

Sin will have no dominion over you,
since you are . . . under grace.
<small>ROMANS 6:14 RSV</small>

❖

[The Lord] sent from on high, He took me;
He drew me out of many waters.
He delivered me from my strong enemy,
And from those who hated me,
for they were too mighty for me.
<small>PSALM 18:16-17 NASB</small>

. . . I will pray.

Dear God,

Even though we, her parents, can't agree about many things, we both want the same thing for our daughter: freedom from these insidious addictions. At first, we thought her lengthy unexplained absences simply meant she was becoming more grown-up and independent. Now we know better. In fact, we know too much, and it interferes with our ability to trust her to You.

We wish we could push a redial button and start everything afresh. Quite possibly, she does too, although we can't tell by her attitude.

If we were wealthy enough to buy our way out of this, we know even that wouldn't work. Neither is it possible, even with the help of the "experts," to make her change her self-destructive ways.

She's been gone longer than she ever has been before. She's out there somewhere. You know where she is. Send angels to protect her and persuade her to come home to us and to You.

We bow our tear-stained faces before You, Lord. Come as a Warrior to do battle with the enemies into whose camp our daughter has wandered. We pray in Jesus' strong name.

Amin.

Amen.

❋

Father, set me free in the glory of thy will, so that
I will only as thou willest. . . . Thou alone art
deliverance—absolute safety from every cause and
kind of trouble that ever existed, anywhere now exists,
or ever can exist in thy universe.

George MacDonald

When my child is dealing with conflict . . .

Don't repay evil for evil. Don't retaliate when people say unkind things about you. Instead, pay them back with a blessing. That is what God wants you to do, and he will bless you for it. For the Scriptures say, "If you want a happy life and good days, keep your tongue from speaking evil, and keep your lips from telling lies. Turn away from evil and do good. Work hard at living in peace with others. The eyes of the Lord watch over those who do right, and his ears are open to their prayers."

1 PETER 3:9-12 NLT

✤

Christ, who suffered for you, is your example. Follow in his steps. He never sinned, and he never deceived anyone. He did not retaliate when he was insulted. When he suffered, he did not threaten to get even. He left his case in the hands of God, who always judges fairly.

1 PETER 2:21-23 NLT

✤

Trust GOD from the bottom of your heart; don't try to figure out everything on your own. Listen for GOD's voice in everything you do, everywhere you go; he's the one who will keep you on track.

PROVERBS 3:5-6 MSG

. . . I will pray.

Loving Lord,

An ordinary argument threatens to become a big deal, and I'm running to You in prayer about it. These arguments have happened before, and the other times they didn't work out very well. I'm hoping this time will be different if I pray about it.

There are two parts to my prayer: Please give me wisdom to know what to do. And please don't let this childish conflict turn into a war of words between two sets of parents. I would like to see the kids work it out themselves rather than run from it or make it worse. I would like to see a change for the better in their relationship.

Help me to model forgiveness and peacemaking while not teaching my son to become a doormat. Keep him from developing a hard heart and from learning contentious patterns or self-protective tactics.

In the heat of the moment, it's so hard to remember that You are the Helper and that You are right there beside us in every situation. Please remind me that You are close by, so I can remind my son.

Amen.

❊

Don't let controversy hurt your soul. Live near to God by prayer. Just fall down at His feet and open your very soul before Him, and throw yourself right into His arms.

Catherine Booth

When my child is in danger . . .

The eternal God is thy refuge, and underneath are the everlasting arms: and he shall thrust out the enemy from before thee; and shall say, Destroy them.
DEUTERONOMY 33:27 KJV

❖

The LORD answer you in the day of trouble!
The name of the God of Jacob protect you!
PSALM 20:1 RSV

❖

When they had gone, an angel of the Lord appeared to Joseph in a dream. "Get up," he said, "take the child and his mother and escape to Egypt. Stay there until I tell you, for Herod is going to search for the child to kill him."
MATTHEW 2:13

❖

Let all who take refuge in you rejoice;
let them ever sing for joy.
Spread your protection over them.
PSALM 5:11 NRSV

. . . I will pray.

Father God,

The older my daughter gets, the more I'm aware of the dangers out there. It's not only sicknesses or accidents or evil people, it's the multitude of dangers that involve her own immature decisions. It doesn't seem very simple to protect her from herself. The situation is always changing.

But I don't believe You are changing. You are still her Protector, and You still answer the prayers of a parent who worries about the risks her precious daughter faces. I ask You to send Your angels to protect my daughter. Drive away the forces of evil that lurk in the shadows. Preserve her life and protect her well-being. Hide her in Your impenetrable stronghold and drown out the tempter's voice. My daughter is so susceptible to peer pressure. I ask You to direct her feet away from paths that lead to destruction—even if her friends invite her to follow them.

Protect her body, her mind, her spirit. I cannot be sure of the future, but I am confident that You are holding it. Don't let go, Lord. Keep my child in the hollow of Your hand.

Amen.

❧

Believing God's promises,
the Christian is taken through difficulties
of every shape and size—and arrives safely.
Richard C. Halverson

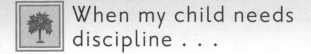

When my child needs discipline . . .

Intelligent children listen to their parents;
foolish children do their own thing. . . .
A refusal to correct is a refusal to love;
love your children by disciplining them.
PROVERBS 13:1,24 MSG

❖

Discipline your children while you still have the chance;
indulging them destroys them.
PROVERBS 19:18 MSG

❖

Discipline always seems painful rather than pleasant at the
time, but later it yields the peaceful fruit of righteousness to
those who have been trained by it.
HEBREWS 12:11 NRSV

❖

The LORD corrects those he loves,
just as parents correct the child they delight in.
PROVERBS 3:12 NCV

. . . I will pray.

Heavenly Father,

You are the one who disciplines each of us in order to keep us from wandering away from You. As a parent to my child, I need to do the same, but it's never easy.

More often than not, I get more upset than I should, expecting somehow that the louder my voice, the better the results. I don't want to fall into that pit this time. So I'm asking You for calmness, for the ability to think straight and to deliver effective, even loving, discipline. Today, may my "rod" of discipline not be a bludgeon.

Instill a bit of Your own heart in mine, Lord. May I reflect Your wonderful combination of unconditional love and firm adherence to what is right. Make it possible for me to keep in mind the goal: a clear pathway to You, one that is not blocked off by sinfulness.

I'm not quite sure what kind of discipline to choose (I'm still in Discipline School myself), so help me with that as well, Lord. From Your heavenly storehouse, I need wisdom, I need grace, I need resolve, and I need peace. I pray that my child's response will be a good one. Thank You in advance.

Amen.

❋

Discipline and love are not antithetical;
one is a function of the other.

James C. Dobson

When my child needs good friends . . .

There are "friends" who destroy each other,
but a real friend sticks closer than a brother.
PROVERBS 18:24 NLT

❖

As iron sharpens iron, a friend sharpens a friend.
PROVERBS 27:17 NLT

❖

Friends love through all kinds of weather.
PROVERBS 17:17 MSG

❖

Two are better than one, because they have a good reward for
their toil. For if they fall, one will lift up the other.
ECCLESIASTES 4:9-10 NRSV

❖

Jonathan made David reaffirm his vow of friendship again,
for Jonathan loved David as much as he loved himself.
1 SAMUEL 20:17 NLT

. . . I will pray.

Dear Lord and Friend,

My prayer today is a simple one: Please provide a friend, or several friends, for my lonely son. I don't know why I never thought to pray for this before.

Help him break out of his well-established pattern of going solo. I can see in his eyes and the slump of his shoulders how much he'd love to be part of a group, or even to be paired with one buddy. The computer isn't a good-enough friend. He needs a real, live one, or more than one.

I know I can't make friends materialize. And I can't push him to try things he's not interested in.

I suppose, though—and, Lord, maybe You just put this idea into my head!—I could model this friend-finding business for him. I could reach out a little more and see if I can make some new friends myself.

May he find his new friends the same way, by reaching out in friendship, by being a friend first. Thank You for modeling that for me. You took the initiative with me. You are a true Friend.

Amen!

❋

A friend is one who knows you as you are,
understands where you've been,
accepts who you've become, and still,
gently invites you to grow.
Author Unknown

When my child needs emotional healing . . .

Arise, cry aloud in the night
At the beginning of the night watches;
Pour out your heart like water
Before the presence of the Lord;
Lift up your hands to Him
For the life of your little ones.
LAMENTATIONS 2:19 NASB

❖

[Jesus said] Blessed are those who mourn,
For they shall be comforted.
MATTHEW 5:4 NKJV

❖

My health fails; my spirits droop, yet God remains!
He is the strength of my heart; he is mine forever!
PSALM 73:26 TLB

❖

Some people like to make cutting remarks,
but the words of the wise soothe and heal.
PROVERBS 12:18 TLB

. . . I will pray.

Precious Lord,

My son's anger is going to get him in trouble someday. The bigger he gets, the more likely it is that he will hurt someone when he lashes out. I'm not wired like that. If there's such a thing as a natural pacifist, that would be me. How did I end up with such a short-tempered child?

Father, I believe that You created my son, that You personally selected and assembled his component parts, including his emotional makeup. And You know everything, so You know how his life circumstances have worked out to date. Surely, some of those have given him cause to be upset.

Still, You know all about him. You're aware of everything he has been through and every challenge he's faced. I ask You, Lord, to touch his heart. Allow him to feel Your love and healing washing over him, cleansing and giving him a new start.

Then, Lord, show me how to help him stay grounded, how to be a good example and a trusted confidante. I commit my child to You, knowing that You will make the difference for him. Thank You for Your love and Your care and Your healing touch.

Amen.

❧

Apt words have power to assuage
The tumors of a troubled mind
And are as balm to fester'd wounds.

John Milton

When my child needs physical healing . . .

One of the leaders of the synagogue named Jairus came and,
when he saw [Jesus], fell at his feet and begged him
repeatedly, "My little daughter is at the point of death.
Come and lay Your hands on her, so that she may be made
well, and live." So [Jesus] went with him. . . . When they
came to the house of the leader of the synagogue . . .
[Jesus] took her by the hand and said to her,
"Talitha cum," which means, "Little girl, get up!"
And immediately the girl got up and began to walk.
MARK 5:22-24,38,41-42 NRSV

❖

When he heard that Jesus had come out of Judea into Galilee,
he went to Him and was imploring Him to come down and
heal his son; for he was at the point of death. . . . Jesus said to
him, "Go; your son lives." The man believed the word that
Jesus spoke to him and started off.
JOHN 4:47,50 NASB

❖

[The Lord Almighty says] For you who revere my name,
the sun of righteousness will rise with healing in its wings.
MALACHI 4:2

. . . I will pray.

Precious Lord,

When You walked this earth, You were known as the Great Physician, the Mighty Healer. You haven't changed. That's why I'm so glad You are here with us this morning. We surely do need Your help. My child is sick, and when something is wrong with my child, everything is wrong with me.

Show me what to do. Give me Your wisdom to know what action to take—if any. Should we head for the doctor's office or just wait for the illness to pass? You know all about these things—a lot more than I do anyway. I'm depending on You. We both are.

As I place my hand on my child's sweet forehead, I'm going to step away and let You do Your work. I know that You won't let us down—whether Your healing is instant or in Your perfect time and Your perfect way. Just as so many other parents did in the Bible, I place my child in Your hands and ask You to be just who You are—kind, loving, merciful, gentle. Heal my sweet one, Lord. My hope is in You.

Amen.

❈

Thy touch hath still its ancient power,
Thy loving touch that healeth all.

Amy Carmichael

When my child is dealing with difficulties at home . . .

Above all these put on love,
which binds everything together in perfect harmony.
COLOSSIANS 3:14 RSV

❈

These words, which I am commanding you today,
shall be on your heart. You shall teach them diligently to your
sons and shall talk of them when you sit in your house
and when you walk by the way and when you
lie down and when you rise up.
DEUTERONOMY 6:6-7 NASB

❈

[Jesus said] If anyone loves Me, he will keep My word;
and My Father will love him, and We will come to him
and make Our home with him.
JOHN 14:23 NKJV

❈

How very good and pleasant it is when kindred
live together in unity! . . . For there the LORD ordained
his blessing, life forevermore.
PSALM 133:1,3 NRSV

. . . I will pray.

Heavenly Father,

Our home is a mess right now. And the strain on my child is showing. I just put him to bed, and he was so sullen he was unwilling even to turn his cheek for a good-night kiss.

What can I do about it? I'm part of the problem, it seems. Truth be told, so is he. We're all part of the problem. Our difficulties began when we first became a family, and I don't think they're going away anytime soon.

Still, I pray with hope that You can and will do something to help. Tonight, I will focus my prayer on my son's behalf. Bless his sleep, Lord, and restore his young soul. Help him to find his true home—the place where You dwell. May he discover that he can be at home with You anyplace, even when trouble has come to roost in the one place that is supposed to be a refuge—his family home.

During this night, wash away the residue of our troubles. Undo the damage of unloving words hastily spoken. Clear the spiritual atmosphere so the emotional atmosphere has a better chance of dawning brighter tomorrow.

You have my love, my devotion, and my thanks, Lord.
Amen.

❈

It is [at home]—with fellow family members—
we hammer out our convictions on the anvil of
relationships. It is there we cultivate the valuable
things in life, like attitudes, memories, beliefs,
and most of all, character.

Charles R. Swindoll

When my child is not in relationship with God . . .

*Train up a child in the way he should go: and when he is old,
he will not depart from it.*

<small>PROVERBS 22:6 KJV</small>

❈

*I am confident of this very thing, that He who began a good
work in you will perfect it until the day of Christ Jesus.*

<small>PHILIPPIANS 1:6 NASB</small>

❈

*God is at work within you, helping you want to obey him,
and then helping you do what he wants.*

<small>PHILIPPIANS 2:13 TLB</small>

❈

*It shall be that whoever calls on the name of the Lord
shall be saved.*

<small>ACTS 2:21 RSV</small>

❈

*The father said, "We must celebrate with a feast, for this son
of mine was dead and has returned to life. He was lost and is
found." So the party began.*

<small>LUKE 15:23-24 TLB</small>

. . . I will pray.

Dear Lord,

I call my child up, so hopeful. "Want to come for dinner Sunday? We'd love to have you go to church with us too!"

Laughter. "Dinner's great, but not church. You know I sleep in on Sundays. Besides, I'm not really into God. I mean, He's okay for you to believe in, but . . . "

The words stab my heart. Dear God, I've tried to bring my child up Your way. Together we went to Your house. Together we learned all about You, Your love, Your power, Your Word, Your laws. What joy it was to have our family united in the Lord!

But then came mocking friends, professors, books. And my child has chosen another way, breaking my heart.

Yet Your Word gives me hope that if I continue both being faithful to You and a loving witness to my child—no tricks, no arguments, no pressure—and let You continue Your witness as well, that one day my child's faith will return.

Father, I'm holding on to that hope, believing that between Your love and mine, my child one day will come home! Home to both of us!

Thank You for Your faithfulness!

Amen.

�֍

Never cease loving a person and never give up hope for him, for even the Prodigal Son who had fallen most low could still be saved.

Søren Kierkegaard

When my child is struggling in school . . .

You made all the delicate, inner parts of my body, and knit them together in my mother's womb. Thank you for making me so wonderfully complex! It is amazing to think about. Your workmanship is marvelous—and how well I know it.
PSALM 139:13-14 TLB

❈

All your . . . children shall be disciples [taught by the Lord . . .], and great shall be the peace and undisturbed composure of your children.
ISAIAH 54:13 AMP

❈

I've even become smarter than my teachers
since I've pondered and absorbed your counsel.
PSALM 119:99 MSG

❈

The LORD *gives wisdom,*
and from his mouth come knowledge and understanding.
PROVERBS 2:6

. . . I will pray.

Heavenly Father,

School is such a struggle for my child and he is miserable. No matter how hard he tries, he seems unable to grasp what is being taught. When he fails, he gets frustrated and thinks he is stupid. And that breaks my heart. He wants to give up, and honestly, right now I'd like to give up too.

But of course I can't do that. Father, I know that You created my child to be a very special individual and that You love him even more than I do. I also know that You have a great plan for his life. Give his teacher and me wisdom and insight into what my child really needs. Maybe he is wired differently from other children. Give us patience and show us methods that will unlock his mind and make learning fun. Help us to discover his bent so that we can nurture it and help him fulfill the destiny for which You created him.

Encourage my child's heart, Father, and help him see that he is a winner. Give him the tenacity to keep on trying and help him succeed.

Amen.

There are no hopeless situations; there are only people who have grown hopeless about them.

Clare Boothe Luce

When my spouse is struggling with addiction . . .

We have escaped with our lives as a bird
from a hunter's snare. The snare is broken and we are free!
Our help is from the Lord.
PSALM 124:7-8 TLB

❊

O Lord, you have freed me from my bonds and
I will serve you forever.
PSALM 116:16 TLB

❊

Wretched man that I am!
Who will set me free from the body of this death?
Thanks be to God through Jesus Christ our Lord!
ROMANS 7:24-25 NASB

❊

[Jesus said] If the Son sets you free, you will be free indeed.
JOHN 8:36

❊

It was for freedom that Christ set us free; therefore keep
standing firm and do not be subject again to a yoke of slavery.
GALATIANS 5:1 NASB

. . . I will pray.

Caring Father,

When we first married, we promised that no one would ever come between us. We never dreamed our worst enemy could be something, rather than someone: addiction.

I've tried ignoring my spouse's problem, hoping it would just go away. I've also begged, cajoled, threatened, screamed, and cried, but nothing has changed. Now I realize that my spouse's problem has become my problem too. I'm at the end of my rope, the end of my hope.

No, You are my hope. And I know that through You I can find the strength I need to quit being an enabler. Lead me to support groups, books, and people that will empower me and give me wisdom in dealing with this addiction. I realize that the only person I can change is me. Give me the tools I need to do that.

Although I cannot change my spouse, You can. Thank You for Your promise that my mate can know the truth—the truth that sets free. And I pray that the same Spirit that raised Christ from the dead will fill my spouse, giving him the power to triumph over addiction, for the one the Son sets free is free indeed.

Amen.

✻

God made us, and God is able to empower us
to do whatever he calls us to do.

Warren W. Wiersbe

When my spouse is dealing with conflict . . .

We are not fighting against people made of flesh and blood,
but against the evil rulers and authorities of the unseen world,
against those mighty powers of darkness who rule this world,
and against wicked spirits in the heavenly realms.
EPHESIANS 6:12 NLT

❖

Try to live in peace with everyone; work hard at it.
PSALM 34:14 TLB

❖

Hatred stirs up strife, but love covers all offenses.
PROVERBS 10:12 NRSV

❖

Those who are hot-tempered stir up strife,
but those who are slow to anger calm contention.
PROVERBS 15:18 NRSV

❖

Do not be overcome by evil, but overcome evil with good.
ROMANS 12:21 RSV

. . . I will pray.

Loving Father,

I am concerned about my spouse and the conflict in which she has become involved. Personalities have clashed, feelings have been bruised, and the whole situation is unfair.

Father, You know about this better than any of us. You know the people involved and what is motivating them, and I am asking You to intervene. First I pray for my spouse, that You would comfort and encourage her. Remind her that You love her unconditionally and that You believe in her. Then, give her insight into this other individual—help her to put herself in this other person's shoes and see things from that perspective. Your Word says that we wrestle not with flesh and blood but with spiritual forces that manipulate people. Help my spouse to recognize this. Also help her to let go of the hurt she has suffered and to extend love and forgiveness to this person. Help her to conduct herself the way Jesus would.

I also pray that You will work in the heart of the other person. Help these two to resolve their conflict so that both parties win and they can move on.

Amen.

�֎

In conflict with unholy powers,
We grasp the weapons He has given,
The light and truth and love of heaven.

John Greenleaf Whittier

When my spouse is in danger . . .

During danger he will keep me safe in his shelter.
He will hide me in his Holy Tent,
or he will keep me safe on a high mountain.
PSALM 27:5 NCV

The LORD is your protection;
you have made God Most High your place of safety.
Nothing bad will happen to you;
no disaster will come to your home.
He has put his angels in charge of you
to watch over you wherever you go.
PSALM 91:9-11 NCV

The LORD will protect you from all dangers;
he will guard your life.
PSALM 121:7 NCV

God is our refuge and strength,
a tested help in times of trouble.
PSALM 46:1 TLB

. . . I will pray.

My Dearest Father,

You know that I love my spouse more than life itself and that I would do anything to protect him from harm, just as he tries to protect me.

But what do I do now? My spouse is in danger and it's out of my control. I'm worried. I feel sick. I wish there were no such things as accidents, sickness, crime, war, or natural disasters. But of course they're all very real.

Father, I ask You to send forth angels to protect my mate. Help me to remember that You love my spouse even more than I do. Help me to find peace in knowing that You have been protecting and guiding us both all our lives—indeed, You are the one who brought us together. You promise to be with us everywhere, at all times, even in times of danger, for no danger is too big for You to handle. After all, Your power keeps the entire universe going! You truly have the whole world in Your hands, including—especially including—the love of my life.

Thank You for wrapping both my spouse and me in Your loving arms of protection.

Amen.

✳

Angels are God's secret service agents.
Their assignment—our protection.

Meriwether Williams

When my spouse needs guidance . . .

Let the peace (soul harmony which comes) from Christ
rule (act as umpire continually) in your hearts [deciding and
settling with finality all questions that arise in your minds].
COLOSSIANS 3:15 AMP

❖

Your ears will hear a word behind you,
"This is the way, walk in it."
ISAIAH 30:21 NASB

❖

I am always with you;
You have held my hand.
You guide me with your advice.
PSALM 73:23-24 NCV

❖

This God . . . will be our guide even to the end.
PSALM 48:14

❖

The LORD will guide you continually.
ISAIAH 58:11 RSV

. . . I will pray.

Dear Father,

After filling out a sheet full of pros and cons, my spouse still doesn't know what to do. The two of us make the major decisions for our family: about our children, where to live, what car to buy, where to vacation. But now my loved one has a very important decision to make, a decision I can't make for her.

I pray that You will replace the anxiety she is feeling with Your peace. I pray that she will be able to cast her care on You and be mindful that she is not alone—that You are with her, holding her hand.

You promise in Your Word that You will guide us always, that if we will acknowledge You in all our ways, You will direct our steps. I pray that You will do this for my spouse. As she sits quietly before You, I pray that she will hear Your still, small voice, telling her which way to go. I pray that Your peace will act as an umpire, helping her to decide with finality Your will for the situation.

Thank You for helping us trust You wholly.

Amen.

God is an ever-present Spirit guiding all that happens to a wise and holy end.

David Hume

When my spouse needs emotional healing . . .

O Lord, You brought my soul up from the grave;
You have kept me alive, that I should not go down to the pit.
PSALM 30:3 NKJV

❉

He healeth the broken in heart, and bindeth up their wounds.
PSALM 147:3 KJV

❉

To all who mourn in Israel, he will give beauty for ashes,
joy instead of mourning, praise instead of despair.
ISAIAH 61:3 NLT

❉

I will exalt you, O Lord,
for you lifted me out of the depths.
PSALM 30:1

❉

The eternal God is your Refuge,
And underneath are the everlasting arms.
DEUTERONOMY 33:27 TLB

. . . I will pray.

My Dear Lord,

The title of the song "Stormy Weather" describes what my spouse is experiencing. Dark clouds of depression and pain hang heavy and have closed in. My loved one's heart is emotionally torn up, crushed by a pain almost too great to express. And because my spouse hurts, so do I. After all, You have made us to be one.

I'm miserable that I can't find a way to bring my loved one the comfort I long to provide. Just talking it out or pretending nothing's wrong hasn't worked. And the wound is too deep for me just to "kiss it and make it all better."

But no pain is too deep or great for You.

O God of all compassion and comfort, hold my loved one in Your arms. Touch those wounded emotions and bring healing, wholeness. Guide us as we seek help together—through books, our pastor, a counselor, a psychologist, or someone else You might lead us to. If a change of scenery would help, let us know and we will go.

Thank You for walking with us through this difficult time. May it bring us even closer to You.

Amen.

❋

God can do wonders with a broken heart—
if we give him all of the pieces.
Author Unknown

When my spouse needs physical healing . . .

"I will restore you to health
and heal your wounds,"
declares the LORD.
JEREMIAH 30:17

❖

Everyone was trying to touch [Jesus], for when they did
healing power went out from him and they were cured.
LUKE 6:19 TLB

❖

Praise the LORD, O my soul,
and forget not all his benefits—
. . . who heals all your diseases.
PSALM 103:2-3

❖

O LORD, heal me, for my bones are in agony.
My soul is in anguish.
PSALM 6:2-3

. . . I will pray.

O Great Physician,

Illness is so hard on us adults, so inconvenient. Whether it is serious enough to put us in the hospital or just a simple head cold, sickness interrupts our lives, makes us miserable, prevents our doing our best work, hinders our taking care of responsibilities, and keeps us from doing all of the things we want to do. But this is where my spouse is—in need of physical healing.

I bring my sweetheart to You in prayer because Jesus is the Great Physician. I believe Your Word that says, "By His stripes, we are healed." I embrace this promise for my spouse. I pray for the doctors and medical personnel, that You would give them wisdom and insight into my spouse's condition and reveal to them the best course of action. I pray that any medication my spouse takes will do what it is designed to do and not cause any negative side effects. Help my spouse to get adequate rest and to do all that is necessary to expedite the healing process.

All healing comes from You, Father, and I thank and praise You in advance for restoring health to my spouse.

Amen.

❉

Health is a state of complete physical, mental, and social well-being.
The World Health Organization

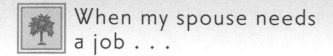

When my spouse needs a job . . .

The human mind plans the way,
but the LORD directs the steps.
PROVERBS 16:9 NRSV

❧

In all your ways acknowledge Him,
And He will make your paths straight.
PROVERBS 3:6 NASB

❧

God wants all people to eat and drink and be happy in their
work, which are gifts from God.
ECCLESIASTES 3:13 NCV

❧

Man goes forth to his work
And to his labor until evening.
PSALM 104:23 NASB

❧

[Jesus said] Give us this day our daily bread.
MATTHEW 6:11 NASB

. . . I will pray.

Dear Lord,

Out of work—the fear of everyone in the labor force. Why has this happened? What are we going to do? This is a scary place for both of us. You know we need finances for food, housing, and all of our other necessities. I'm trying not to panic, but I need Your help to keep my eyes on You and Your promises to provide for us.

As my spouse diligently goes through the want ads, sends out résumés, and responds to "Help Wanted" signs, I ask You to guide his steps. Networking is always important, so I ask You to lead people across our paths who could connect us to other people and opportunities.

Could it be that You have something totally different for us, such as going into a different field, returning to school, or moving to a new location? We are open to checking all our options, doing research on the Internet, and investigating any and all ideas.

One thing we're sure of: we know You have good plans for us. Wherever we go and whatever we do, we want Your help!

Thank You!

Amen.

❋

Work is not a curse, it is a blessing from God
who calls man to rule the earth and transform it.

John Paul II

When my spouse is not in relationship with God . . .

Your godly lives will speak to them better than any words.
They will be won over by watching your pure, godly behavior.
1 PETER 3:1-2 NLT

❧

If any believer has a wife who is an unbeliever, and she
consents to live with him, he should not divorce her. And if
any woman has a husband who is an unbeliever, and he
consents to live with her, she should not divorce him. For the
unbelieving husband is made holy through his wife, and the
unbelieving wife is made holy through her husband.
1 CORINTHIANS 7:12-14 NRSV

❧

[The jailer] brought [Paul and Silas] out and begged them,
"Sirs, what must I do to be saved?" They replied,
"Believe on the Lord Jesus and you will be saved,
and your entire household."
ACTS 16:30-31 TLB

❧

[Joshua said] As for me and my house,
we will serve the LORD.
JOSHUA 24:15 RSV

. . . I will pray.

Dear God of Love,

I love my spouse with all my heart. I love You with all my heart too. The problem? The one I love loves me—but he does not share my love for You.

Sure, once in a while we go to church together—mostly at Easter or Christmas or for a wedding. But the rest of the time we go our separate ways on Sunday mornings. If I feel guilty leaving him and stay home, I'm miserable that I'm missing out on Your praise, Your Word, and fellowship with Your children.

Will we never be able to pray and rejoice in You together? I want my spouse to know You the way I do. And what about after this life—I can't even stand the thought of our being apart throughout all eternity!

Yet, dear Lord, as I look through the Bible, I see so many promises that if I'm faithful to You and also faithfully loving to my spouse, there is hope that one day my loved one will turn to You and become Your child as well.

That's the power of love. I believe in that power. Thank You for Your promises.

Amen.

✤

If you live by the same values and priorities [Jesus] had, you will find evangelism happening naturally. It becomes a lifestyle and not a project.

Rebecca Manley Pippert

When my spouse is unfaithful . . .

[Jesus said] He hath sent me to heal the brokenhearted.
LUKE 4:18 KJV

❈

[Jesus said] When you pray, you should pray like this:
"Our Father in heaven. . . . Forgive us for our sins,
just as we have forgiven those who sinned against us."
MATTHEW 6:9,12 NCV

❈

[Jesus said] Whenever you stand praying, forgive, if you have
anything against any one; so that your Father also who is in
heaven may forgive you your trespasses.
MARK 11:25 RSV

❈

Forgive as quickly and completely as the Master forgave you.
COLOSSIANS 3:13 MSG

. . . I will pray.

My Father,

At our wedding, we both vowed to "cleave" only to each other. But something's happened—something terrible. My spouse has been unfaithful.

I'm shocked, furious, insulted, humiliated, devastated, heartbroken. Now what? Do I storm out and file for divorce? Should I try to go on as if nothing's happened? If I stay, will I always be suspicious of every phone call, e-mail, late night at work?

If I don't tell my friends, will they find out anyway? I'm sure they'd advise everything from staying to leaving.

But Your Word does advise me to seek "counselors," and not just my friends—qualified advisors, such as my pastor or a licensed marriage counselor. If my spouse goes with me, maybe we can find out what went wrong between us and how we can build a new life together.

And if my spouse refuses? I can go by myself. Maybe my counselor can inform me of a support group. I want to keep the door open to reconciliation. But I also need to know what my options are if that's not possible.

There's a painful journey ahead, Lord. Thank You for holding my hand.

Amen.

❋

It takes two sides to make a lasting peace,
but it only takes one to make the first step.

Edward M. Kennedy

When my spouse has concerns at work . . .

A gentle answer turns away wrath,
but harsh words cause quarrels.
PROVERBS 15:1 TLB

❈

[Jesus said,] "Blessed are the peacemakers:
for they shall be called the children of God."
MATTHEW 5:9 KJV

❈

[Jesus said] The laborer deserves his wages.
LUKE 10:7 RSV

❈

Servants, respectfully obey your earthly masters but always
with an eye to obeying the real master, Christ. Don't just do
what you have to do to get by, but work heartily, as Christ's
servants doing what God wants you to do. And work with a
smile on your face, always keeping in mind that no matter
who happens to be giving the orders, you're really serving
God. Good work will get you good pay from the Master,
regardless of whether you are slave or free.
EPHESIANS 6:5-8 MSG

. . . I will pray.

Dear Lord,

We work overtime, eat lunch at our desks, and keep going despite setbacks, because we want to do our very best at work. We want to be proud of our paychecks and rejoice that we can provide for our families.

You know that my spouse has always given 110 percent, taking pride in doing the finest job possible. But work also involves other people—customers, coworkers, and bosses. When everyone is courteous, upbeat, and helpful, that is fine. But when taunts, racial slurs, insults, power cliques, addictions, embezzlement, even sexual harassment arise, the workplace becomes a battlefield. And the work still has to be done!

Father, please go before my loved one each day, granting courage and self-control to give a quiet answer when suffering injustice. Help my spouse to explore ways to defuse the situation—such as talking to the boss, confiding in human resources, taking someone out to lunch to talk one-on-one, using humor to turn threats into laughter. And also give my spouse the wisdom to know if and when the situation is impossible to change and the time has come to seek another position—one of Your choosing.

Thank You for Your faithfulness.

Amen.

✻

He that wrestles with us strengthens
our nerves and sharpens our skill.
Our antagonist is our helper.

Edmund Burke

When my spouse needs wisdom . . .

The LORD gives wisdom;
From His mouth come knowledge and understanding.
PROVERBS 2:6 NKJV

❖

You teach me wisdom in the inmost place.
PSALM 51:6

❖

If any of you is lacking in wisdom, ask God, who gives to all
generously and ungrudgingly, and it will be given you.
JAMES 1:5 NRSV

❖

The fear of the LORD is the beginning of wisdom;
a good understanding have all those who practice it.
PSALM 111:10 RSV

❖

The mouth of the righteous brings forth wisdom.
PROVERBS 10:31 RSV

. . . I will pray.

Dearest Father,

"If only I knew the answer!" That's what my spouse said tonight.

No, not to a math quiz or knock-knock joke or trivia question, but to a very real and important dilemma. The kind that makes the difference between being stuck and going forward, between turmoil and peace, between right and wrong. A lot is riding on this, and it is causing a great deal of anxiety.

If I knew the magic words that would settle this, I would say them. Unfortunately, I don't. I want to solve the problem, but I can't. It's so hard for me not to be able to fix this!

What I can do is look to You and pray on behalf of the love of my life. You are the only all-wise one, the source of the wisest, best answers. Please help my spouse to have a heart attuned to hear those answers, to understand Your direction—plus the courage to take Your advice.

And please help me be ready to do whatever is necessary to support my loved one in this. Help us make wise decisions together with Your help.

Thank You.

Amen.

❉

Don't expect wisdom to come into your life like
great chunks of rock on a conveyor belt. . . .
Wisdom comes privately from God as a by-product of
right decisions, godly reactions, and the application of
spiritual principles to daily circumstances.

Charles R. Swindoll

When my friend or family member is struggling with addiction . . .

Is not this the fast that I have chosen?
To loose the bands of wickedness, to undo the heavy burdens,
and to let the oppressed go free?
ISAIAH 58:6 KJV

✤

[Jesus said] You will know the truth,
and the truth will make you free.
JOHN 8:32 NASB

✤

[Jesus said]
The Spirit of the Lord is upon me. . . .
He has sent me to proclaim
that captives will be released.
LUKE 4:18 NLT

✤

Our old sinful selves were crucified with Christ so that
sin might lose its power in our lives. We are no longer slaves
to sin. For when we died with Christ we were set free
from the power of sin.
ROMANS 6:6-7 NLT

. . . I will pray.

My Lord,

I am so concerned. Addiction has swallowed up someone I love, turning a once-sunny personality into a volatile one, a previously healthy body into a nervous wreck.

So many of her friends and family—especially the ones who live far away—are in denial over the changes that are taking place, but I can see things going from bad to worse. What a tragedy! Addiction ruins homes, marriages, financial credit, and careers. It destroys health, fosters crime—even murder.

What can I do? I know that I cannot control this individual, but I don't want to be an enabler. Talking has produced nothing but empty promises. Should I talk to other significant people in this person's life? Perhaps if we coordinated our efforts, we could organize an intervention to motivate our loved one to seek help. I want to see this bondage broken before it is too late.

I realize that You love this individual even more than I do and that Jesus defeated the power of addiction when He was raised from the dead. I entrust this precious person to Your care.

Amen.

❋

Freedom is a gift from heaven.
Denis Diderot

When my friend or family member is dealing with conflict . . .

Now the God of peace, who brought up from the dead the great Shepherd of the sheep through the blood of the eternal covenant, even Jesus our Lord, equip you in every good thing to do His will, working in us that which is pleasing in His sight, through Jesus Christ.
HEBREWS 13:20-21 NASB

❊

Counselors of peace have joy.
PROVERBS 12:20 NKJV

❊

The God of peace will soon crush Satan under your feet.
ROMANS 16:20 NASB

❊

God is not a God of confusion but a God of peace.
1 CORINTHIANS 14:33 NCV

❊

[Paul said] Whatever you have learned or received or heard from me, or seen in me—put it into practice. And the God of peace will be with you.
PHILIPPIANS 4:9

. . . I will pray.

Dearest Lord,

Why do people fight? Why do they quarrel and make snide remarks and gossip? Why do family members and friends jump on each other as if they were sworn enemies—when instead they should be each other's best supporters? Then there are also conflicts in the workplace—resulting in hours of misery instead of joyful productivity. Conflicting ideas, principles, policies, and politics cause people to clash, weakening the entire organization. With everyone thinking his or her own side is right, no one wins.

Someone I know is troubled by such a conflict. And it's breaking my heart to see how it's pulling this dear one down. I ask You to provide strength, comfort, and reassurance. I can always lend an open ear, and I ask You to give me wisdom and insight into the situation so that I can provide encouragement. If You want me to get more directly involved, I am willing. Or if my part is to simply continue to pray, I'll be faithful to do that.

Father, You are the God of peace, and I ask You to guide all parties involved to resolve this situation so that all sides win.

Amen.

❖

Another way to get rid of an enemy is to turn him into a friend.

Author Unknown

When my friend or family member is in danger . . .

Pray that we may be delivered from wicked and evil men. . . .
The Lord is faithful, and he will strengthen and protect you
from the evil one.

2 THESSALONIANS 3:2-3

❊

The LORD loves those who hate evil;
he preserves the lives of his saints;
he delivers them from the hand of the wicked.

PSALM 97:10 RSV

❊

God's angel sets up a circle
of protection around us while we pray.

PSALM 34:7 MSG

❊

He did deliver us from mortal danger. And we are confident
that he will continue to deliver us. He will rescue us because
you are helping by praying for us. As a result, many
will give thanks to God because so many people's prayers
for our safety have been answered.

2 CORINTHIANS 1:10-11 NLT

. . . I will pray.

Heavenly Father,

I'm so thankful for the angels that You've commissioned to watch over and protect us. Danger seems to surround us on every hand: car accidents, plane crashes, train wrecks, terrorist attacks, poisonings, disease, drownings, street muggings, natural disasters, even war.

Someone I care for deeply is in danger right now. Of course, You already know that, just as You know everything. But my stomach is tied in knots, I feel so helpless. I lie awake at night, fearing the worst. I can only imagine the fear this loved one is dealing with!

O Father, release us from our fears and fill our hearts with peace! I know You have the whole world in Your hands—that not even a little sparrow can fall without Your noticing it. I know that there's nowhere in this world that we can be without Your being there also. Yet I'm so used to worrying. I need Your grace to let go and let You take over.

I trust You to be with and deliver this loved one from danger, back to our waiting arms and hearts. I love You so much.

Amen.

❄

The angels are the dispensers and administrators of the divine beneficence toward us; they regard our safety, undertake our defense, direct our ways, and exercise a constant solicitude that no evil befall us.

John Calvin

When my friend or family member goes through divorce . . .

The LORD has anointed me
To bring good news to the afflicted;
He has sent me to bind up the brokenhearted, . . .
To comfort all who mourn.
ISAIAH 61:1-2 NASB

✻

The Lord God has given me his words of wisdom so that I may know what I should say to all these weary ones. Morning by morning he wakens me and opens my understanding to his will.
ISAIAH 50:4 TLB

✻

The word of the LORD came to [Isaiah]: I have heard your prayer, I have seen your tears; behold, I will heal you.
2 KINGS 20:4-5 RSV

✻

God shall wipe away all tears from their eyes.
REVELATION 7:17 KJV

. . . I will pray.

Dearest Lord,

What joy there was to see them so in love. We all agreed it was a match made in heaven.

But now the impossible has happened. Their perfect love story has had a terrible ending. They have filed for divorce.

Divorce is always so tragic. It becomes "he said," "she said"; "he did," "she did"—words spoken in haste and not apologized for. Pride and anger and jealousy and coldness of heart all slowly erode away the tenderness and laughter, leaving broken hearts and broken homes.

Now what? If the divorce is one-sided, how can I best support the injured party without becoming bitter myself? How do we keep channels of communication open to all concerned, such as children, siblings, grandparents, and grandchildren? What advice do I give? If there is still a possibility of reconciliation, help me to encourage it. If not, help me support these I care about in making changes and getting on with their lives.

Father, please let me be a vessel of Your love to pour out on these hurting hearts. Thank You.

Amen.

❖

How shall we comfort those who weep?
By weeping with them.
Father Yelchaninov

When my friend or family member is struggling with finances . . .

Even strong young lions sometimes go hungry,
but those who trust the LORD will never lack any good thing.
PSALM 34:10 NLT

❋

[The Lord said]
This is my resting place forever;
here I will reside, for I have desired it.
I will abundantly bless its provisions;
I will satisfy its poor with bread.
PSALM 132:14-15 NRSV

❋

I was young, and now I am old,
but I have never seen good people left helpless
or their children begging for food.
PSALM 37:25 NCV

❋

God can give you more blessings than you need.
Then you will always have plenty.
2 CORINTHIANS 9:8 NCV

. . . I will pray.

O Father,

Someone I care for has lost all joy. Why? Because of financial hardship. Whether some catastrophic event, the loss of a job, being overextended and in debt, or simply not making enough on the job has caused it, money trouble can squeeze the very life out of its victim. And this is what has happened to one I love. My heart aches over this sad situation.

Will this cause the loss of a car, a home, good credit, even a marriage? Father, You promise to supply all our needs according to Your riches in glory, and I ask that You do this for my loved one.

Help me be a comfort at this time, without prying or condemning. Show me scriptures I can share that will bring hope and encouragement. If this difficulty is self-inflicted, impart wisdom and insight so that my loved one can learn and make changes so this won't happen again. Bring information to light that will help this person chart a new course financially.

Father, I am limited in the amount of help I can provide, but You are not! Thank You for being an unlimited source of supply.

Amen.

❖

The difficulties, hardships, and trials of life,
the obstacles one encounters on the road to fortune,
are positive blessings. They knit the muscles more
firmly, and teach self-reliance.

William Mathews

When my friend or family member is experiencing grief . . .

He was despised and forsaken of men,
A man of sorrows and acquainted with grief; . . .
Surely our griefs He Himself bore,
And our sorrows He carried.
ISAIAH 53:3-4 NASB

❖

Blessed be the God . . . of all comfort, who comforts us in
all our tribulation, that we may be able to comfort those who
are in any trouble, with the comfort with which we ourselves
are comforted by God.
2 CORINTHIANS 1:3-4 NKJV

❖

The Lord has comforted his people,
and will have compassion upon them in their sorrow.
ISAIAH 49:13 TLB

❖

To all who mourn in Israel he will give: Beauty for ashes; joy
instead of mourning; praise instead of heaviness. For God has
planted them like strong and graceful oaks for his own glory.
ISAIAH 61:3 TLB

. . . I will pray.

Dearest Lord,

How can a heart be broken—and still beat?

This is the sad state of someone I care for, who suffers a loss as deep as a grievous wound.

"Is there any way I can help you?" I want to ask. But the words I think of seem so inadequate, almost a mockery of such grief. I send cards and flowers. I call. What else can I do or say?

When I myself am grieving, the cards and flowers I receive so wonderfully comfort me! How I treasure having a friend or loved one willing to listen when I'm ready to talk. How I need the hugs and time spent with someone who cares enough to keep me from being overwhelmed by my despair. How I also appreciate Your love, Your constant presence, Your never-ending comfort at such sad times.

So, please, Lord, help me be a true friend and comforter to this one who is sorrowing now. Help my eyes, ears, arms be available all along this sad journey—and also when healing begins.

Help me direct this sorrowful one to Your ever-open arms.

Amen.

✳

Give sorrow words: the grief that does not speak whispers the o'er-fraught heart, and bids it break.

William Shakespeare

When my friend or family member needs guidance . . .

I will instruct you (says the Lord) and
guide you along the best pathway for your life;
I will advise you and watch your progress.
PSALM 32:8 TLB

✻

[Jesus said] When he, the Spirit of truth, comes,
he will guide you into all truth.
JOHN 16:13

✻

The dayspring from on high hath visited us, to give light to
them that sit in darkness and in the shadow of death, to guide
our feet into the way of peace.
LUKE 1:78-79 KJV

✻

Where there is no guidance the people fall,
But in abundance of counselors there is victory.
PROVERBS 11:14 NASB

✻

The LORD of hosts . . . is wonderful in counsel and
excellent in guidance.
ISAIAH 28:29 NKJV

. . . I will pray.

Dearest Lord,

It would be wonderful if hospitals presented new babies with owners' manuals. Everything from then on would be cut-and-dried: feed, change diaper, put to bed, repeat.

But life, of course, isn't cut-and-dried. It can get very messy and confusing and worrisome. What should be our goals? Where do we go from here? What if we make the wrong decisions?

That's the predicament that the one I care for is in right now. Decisions, decisions, decisions—so many of them to make, some with long-standing consequences.

How can I best help my loved one at this crucial time? Should I offer advice? If so, give me a wise answer, one backed up by the ultimate manual—Your Word. Help me to have listening ears and a listening heart to help understand the real problem. If counsel from experts is in order, lead my loved one to a pastor, doctor, psychologist, career planner, or whoever might offer sound guidance. Perhaps research on the Internet might even help.

Please guide this individual to Your answers, Your decisions, because they are born from Your love and are exactly what my loved one needs. Thank You.

Amen.

❋

It isn't enough to make sure you're on the right track;
you must also make sure you're not going
in the wrong direction.
Author Unknown

When my friend or family member needs emotional healing . . .

[The Lord] turned my sorrow into joy! He took away my clothes of mourning and gave me gay and festive garments to rejoice in so that I might sing glad praises to the Lord instead of lying in silence in the grave.
PSALM 30:11-12 TLB

✥

*Anxiety in the heart of man causes depression,
But a good word makes it glad.*
PROVERBS 12:25 NKJV

✥

They brought to [Jesus] all sick people who were afflicted with . . . torments, . . . and He healed them.
MATTHEW 4:24 NKJV

✥

*Floods of sorrow pour upon me like a thundering cataract.
Yet day by day the Lord also pours out his steadfast love upon me, and through the night I sing his songs and pray to God who gives me life.*
PSALM 42:7-8 TLB

. . . I will pray.

My Father,

We're driving down the highway, enjoying the scenery, when—bam! We encounter a detour sign and are brought to a complete standstill.

That's the way life is right now for someone You and I both care for. Everything seemed normal, zooming along on cruise control, when out of nowhere arose a roadblock. Not on the highway, but inside this one's mind and heart, bringing great anguish and emotional distress. Now, all sense of direction seems lost, as if getting back onto life's highway is completely beyond reach.

Father, some people call this being weak. "Buck up," they say. "Get over it." Or even, "What's the matter? Aren't you trusting God?" But You don't condemn, dear Lord. You've made us and understand that emotions are a very real and necessary part of our lives. Indeed, You Yourself are a God of love, joy, concern, compassion, and tenderness.

Please help me be a source of support and understanding at this time. And if depression and despair seem overpowering, help me direct this tortured one to expert help—a pastor, grief counselor, psychologist, or another person of Your choosing.

Hold us both close in Your wonderful arms! Thank You.

Amen.

How sweet the name of Jesus sounds
In a believer's ear! It soothes his sorrows, heals his wounds, And drives away his fear!

John Newton

When my friend or family member needs physical healing . . .

He himself bore our sins in his body on the tree,
that we might die to sin and live to righteousness.
By his wounds you have been healed.

1 PETER 2:24 RSV

❧

[The Lord says] For you who honor me, goodness will shine
on you like the sun, with healing in its rays.

MALACHI 4:2 NCV

❧

No doubt you know that God anointed Jesus of Nazareth
with the Holy Spirit and with power. Then Jesus went
around doing good and healing all who were oppressed by the
Devil, for God was with him.

ACTS 10:38 NLT

❧

O LORD my God,
I cried to You for help, and You healed me.

PSALM 30:2 NASB

. . . I will pray.

Dearest Lord,

One I care for is critically ill and has asked me to pray. I'm so thankful for the marvelous medical advances we have today, yet even those are sometimes not enough. A multitude of illnesses can still interrupt people's lives and leave them with huge medical expenses, loss of jobs, even death.

So, dear Lord, how best can I support my loved one at this time? Yes, I will call and visit. When possible, I will take casseroles and jokes and news and books and long, warm hugs.

But still, I need something more. I need You with me every minute, giving me encouraging words to share. This sick one needs You moment by moment as well so that we can talk and pray together about You and Your healing; Your love, joy, and peace; and about Your Son, Jesus, and heaven. Yes, even if this patient has never stopped to think much about You before.

Father, I so want my loved one to be healed, but if it isn't to be, help us to make the most of this time together. Hold us close! Thank You.

Amen.

The best of healers is good cheer.

Pindar

When my friend or family member has a problem with infertility . . .

In bitterness of soul Hannah wept much and prayed to the
LORD. And she made a vow, saying, "O LORD Almighty,
if you will only look upon your servant's misery and
remember me, and not forget your servant but give her
a son, then I will give him to the LORD for all the days
of his life." . . . Elkanah lay with Hannah his wife,
and the LORD remembered her. So in the course of time
Hannah conceived and gave birth to a son.
1 SAMUEL 1:10-11,19-20

❊

He settles the barren woman in her home
as a happy mother of children.
PSALM 113:9

❊

[The angel said to Mary] Your relative Elizabeth has . . .
conceived a son in her old age; and she who was called barren
is now in her sixth month. For nothing will be
impossible with God.
LUKE 1:36-37 NASB

. . . I will pray.

Loving Father,

"First comes love, then comes marriage, then comes baby in a baby carriage," goes the old playground chant. But what if the baby carriage, cradle, and aching arms stay empty month after month, year after year?

That's the sad case with a couple I love. They have been so eager to complete their home with an armful of gurgles and goos. They have prayed for this miracle, but the lullabies remain unsung. They wonder if You hear, if You care, if their prayers will ever be answered.

Father, I ask that You help this couple to be open to the many options available today, including fertility treatments and adoption. The Bible tells of Your filling Hannah's and Sarai's empty arms with children of their own, despite seemingly impossible circumstances. Today, children are being adopted from all over the world. Could it be Your plan for this couple to become foster parents to little ones starving for love and security?

This situation is very difficult emotionally. Help me and the other people in this couple's life to support these would-be parents and show them love.

Amen.

❁

Of all created things, the loveliest
and most divine are children.

William Canton

When my friend or family member is not in relationship with God . . .

I will give them an heart to know me, that I am the LORD:
and they shall be my people, and I will be their God.

JEREMIAH 24:7 KJV

❖

"People will no longer have to teach their neighbors
and relatives to know the LORD,
because all people will know me,
from the least to the most important," says the LORD.

JEREMIAH 31:34 NCV

❖

[The Lord God says] The nations will know me when they
see me prove how holy I am in what I do through you.

EZEKIEL 38:16 NCV

❖

[The Lord said] I have loved you with an everlasting love;
Therefore with lovingkindness I have drawn you.

JEREMIAH 31:3 NKJV

. . . I will pray.

O Wonderful Counselor,

Imagining life without You is like imagining a cone without ice cream. You're with me in my happiest moments and my saddest ones, through the bustle of every day and the silence of the night. You bring me joy and peace and encouragement.

My Christian friends understand this. But other friends and family don't. Oh, they may believe in You as a Creator, but they don't want You in their lives; they'd rather run them their own way. Others don't even want to acknowledge that You exist.

I am concerned about one person in particular now. I don't want to nag or preach because that is such a turnoff, but I am willing to share the gospel as You lead. Give me words that will draw this one close to You, and reveal Your love through me. Give me creative ideas that will be effective in winning this one over to You.

This is a big order—but You are a big God, loving this person even more than I do. I thank You for what You are going to do in this precious life.

Amen.

�֍

Being an extrovert isn't essential to evangelism—
obedience and love are.

Rebecca Manley Pippert

When my church needs to be strengthened . . .

How lovely is thy dwelling place, O LORD of hosts! My soul longs, yea, faints for the courts of the LORD; my heart and flesh sing for joy to the living God. . . . Blessed are those who dwell in thy house, ever singing thy praise!

PSALM 84:1-2,4 RSV

❖

Let us not give up meeting together, as some are in the habit of doing, but let us encourage one another—and all the more as you see the Day approaching.

HEBREWS 10:25

❖

It is good and pleasant when God's people live together in peace!

PSALM 133:1 NCV

❖

Is there any encouragement from belonging to Christ? Any comfort from his love? Any fellowship together in the Spirit? Are your hearts tender and sympathetic? Then make me truly happy by agreeing wholeheartedly with each other, loving one another, and working together with one heart and purpose.

PHILIPPIANS 2:1-2 NLT

. . . I will pray.

Dearest Lord,

I love my church, but sometimes it seems that all we do is bicker. Opinions differ, emotions rise up, angry words start flying, and before we know it, the whole place feels as if it's coming apart at the seams. Just about the time we get one disagreement cleared up, another one pops to the surface. I have to wonder if we are accomplishing anything at all of eternal value.

It's all so discouraging. Sometimes I feel like staying home and giving up!

And then I remember how much You love Your Church—enough to have sent Your Son to die for us. So I get up and go to Your house of worship anyway. As I enter the doors, I hear songs of Your praise. And as I lift my voice in worship with the other believers, all my sadness and disappointment and worry melt away. In our time of prayer, I thank You for listening to my burdens and for giving me hope. Then when our pastor preaches, I find healing and hope in Your Word.

My worry lines and frowns give way to peace. Even joy. Especially when the service is over, and I find some friends to greet and hug. Not just friends—they're family!

Thank You for being here with us.

Amen.

❁

In her voyage across the ocean of this world,
the Church is like a great ship being pounded by the
waves of life's different stresses. Our duty is not to
abandon ship but to keep her on her course.

Saint Boniface

When my community needs direction and leadership . . .

I urge, then, first of all, that requests, prayers, intercession and thanksgiving be made for everyone—for kings and all those in authority, that we may live peaceful and quiet lives in godliness and holiness.

1 TIMOTHY 2:1-2

❧

When the righteous are in authority, the people rejoice.

PROVERBS 29:2 NKJV

❧

The king's heart is like channels of water in the hand of the LORD; He turns it wherever He wishes.

PROVERBS 21:1 NASB

❧

Unto us a child is born, unto us a son is given: and the government shall be upon his shoulder.

ISAIAH 9:6 KJV

❧

Remind the believers to yield to the authority of rulers and government leaders, to obey them, to be ready to do good.

TITUS 3:1 NCV

. . . I will pray.

Loving Father,

It's so easy to grumble about the potholes in front of my house or the need for a new school in our area. I hear of politicians embezzling public funds and giving favors to the rich. Then there are the problems with water, air, and ground pollution around here that no one wants to acknowledge.

What about the homeless, families without health insurance, people with disabilities and no safety net, our teachers and firemen and police and hospitals and all the rest—those who need adequate pay and staffing? There are so many needs right here on my street and in my community.

But You know about all of this. Oh, Father, I do pray for the leaders of my community, that You would guide them to make wise decisions that will make our community strong. I pray that You would raise up godly leaders who will lead us in righteousness. Remove any corrupt officials as well as those whose policies go against Your Word.

Show me what part I am to play to make my community better; then give me the courage to act.

Amen.

The government is us; we are the government,
you and I.

Theodore Roosevelt

When my employer needs God's favor . . .

[Abraham's servant said] O LORD, the God of my
master Abraham, please grant me success today,
and show lovingkindness to my master.
GENESIS 24:12 NASB

❖

You bless the righteous, O LORD;
You cover them with favor as with a shield.
PSALM 5:12 NRSV

❖

Send me a sign of your favor. When those who hate me see it
they will lose face because you help and comfort me.
PSALM 86:17 TLB

❖

Our power is based on your favor!
PSALM 89:17 TLB

❖

Whoever finds me [Wisdom] finds life,
And obtains favor from the LORD.
PROVERBS 8:35 NKJV

. . . I will pray.

Dear Lord,

How I thank and praise You for my boss. We've had our ups and downs, but overall, this is a great person to work for.

But a problem has arisen. It's not between us, but it's something entirely different, something out of our control—at least out of mine. So many difficulties can arise for managers of both small and large organizations: financing, bureaucracy, personnel incompatibilities, raging greed, hunger for power, infighting, political pressure, lawsuits, changing markets, corporate takeovers, site condemnations, labor strikes, and all the rest—not to mention personal problems affecting family and health.

It hurts me to see my boss so concerned and weighed down by this burden. I pray that You will give my boss wisdom in dealing with this situation and grant him favor with all parties concerned. Dear Father, only You, the all-knowing one, know how to solve this problem. I pray that You would grant my boss supernatural peace and an assurance that You are guiding this to a positive end. Cause everything to work for his good and Your glory.

Thank You.

Amen.

❊

Almighty God, . . . we humbly beseech Thee that we
may always prove ourselves a people mindful of Thy
favor and glad to do Thy will.

George L. Locke

When I see injustice in the world around me . . .

He has told you, O man, what is good;
And what does the LORD require of you
But to do justice, to love kindness,
And to walk humbly with your God?

MICAH 6:8 NASB

❖

The word of the LORD is upright;
and all his work is done in faithfulness.
He loves righteousness and justice;
the earth is full of the steadfast love of the LORD.

PSALM 33:4-5 RSV

❖

Speak up for those who cannot speak for themselves,
for the rights of all who are destitute.
Speak up and judge fairly;
defend the rights of the poor and needy.

PROVERBS 31:8-9

❖

Blessed (Happy, fortunate, to be envied) is he who
considers the weak and the poor; the Lord will deliver him in
the time of evil and trouble.

PSALM 41:1 AMP

. . . I will pray.

Dearest Lord,

Near me are manicured lawns and locked gates of the well-to-do—and a homeless camp. Upscale boutiques overflow with shoppers, while starving people search through dumpsters for scraps. Corporations make millions by sending jobs overseas, throwing their employees out of work. Life seems so unfair sometimes.

God, I know You are even more concerned with justice than I am. Throughout the Bible You show You are always on the side of kindness, support, and helpfulness—whether extending compassion to the sick, crippled, and blind, or taking care of mistreated slaves, orphans, widows, and the poor. You sent Your Son for the worker as well as the CEO, the homeless as well as the millionaire, the gourmet as well as one who is starving.

Help me fight the injustices I see. I want to contribute to and work with organizations that provide for the needy in practical ways, ones that extend Your love and encouragement. Finally, Father, give me courage to stand up for those who are being treated unjustly. I'll try to help them too.

I want to be a vessel of Your love.

Amen.

❋

Justice is conscience, not a personal conscience
but the conscience of the whole of humanity.

Alexander Solzhenitsyn

When my nation needs
direction and leadership . . .

Blessed is the nation whose God is the LORD.
PSALM 33:12 KJV

❉

I help kings to govern and rulers to make fair laws.
PROVERBS 8:15 NCV

❉

When a country is lawless, it has one ruler after another;
but when it is led by a man with understanding and
knowledge, it continues strong.
PROVERBS 28:2 NCV

❉

Loyalty and truth keep a king in power;
he continues to rule if he is loyal.
PROVERBS 20:28 NCV

❉

[The Lord said] If my people who are called by my name
humble themselves, and pray and seek my face, and turn from
their wicked ways, then I will hear from heaven,
and will forgive their sin and heal their land.
2 CHRONICLES 7:14 RSV

. . I will pray.

God of All Nations,

"O beautiful for spacious skies, for amber waves of grain." Yes, I dearly love the land where You placed me. I thank You that here people of any race or background have freedom to think, read, work, and worship You. That we can elect representatives to work together for the good of all of us.

But somehow getting elected seems to transform too many would-be leaders into self-serving politicians. At local, state, and national levels, those with the people's good at heart get drowned out by political machines, private agendas, and megabuck corporations willing to trade cash for laws—sometimes even pretending to put Your stamp of approval on this travesty.

O Father, help me to see through the pretenses and know which way to vote—and how to encourage my friends to vote as well. To not just criticize the status quo or give the situation up as hopeless, but to be willing to let my voice be heard for the right, the true, the just.

Thank You for this wonderful country. Even though it's not perfect, it is blessed by You.

Amen.

❋

Bad officials are elected by good citizens
who do not vote.

George Jean Nathan

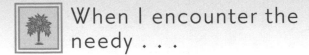

When I encounter the needy . . .

If a brother or sister is naked and lacks daily food, and one of you says to them, "Go in peace; keep warm and eat your fill," and yet you do not supply their bodily needs, what is the good of that? So faith by itself, if it has no works, is dead.

JAMES 2:15-17 NRSV

❖

Blessed are those who help the poor.

PROVERBS 14:21 NLT

❖

If you help the poor, you are lending to the LORD —and he will repay you!

PROVERBS 19:17 NLT

❖

Whoever gives to the poor will lack nothing.

PROVERBS 28:27 NRSV

❖

There will always be poor people in the land. Therefore I command you to be openhanded toward your brothers and toward the poor and needy in your land.

DEUTERONOMY 15:11

. . . I will pray.

Compassionate Father,

On the outside, my refrigerator is full of delightful magnets and to-do lists. On the inside, it is full, period. And still every week I buy more food at the supermarket.

And all the while, pantries and refrigerators in other homes are empty. For even with both parents working, many families today go hungry at least a few days a month between paychecks. Or every day if there are no paychecks at all.

Children need school clothes, school supplies, shoes, and warm winter coats. Their parents need clothes too—and money for heating, water, electric bills, and gas for the family car. Or for riding the bus.

Also, they need to know Your love and truth.

All I have to offer You is my heart, my hands, and my purse. But please take all of them and use them to help these needy people. Whether at a food bank or rescue center or other charitable organization, put my hands and heart to work to warm a heart, fill a stomach, and heal a soul—to be a lighthouse to lead them to You, so they can love You as I do.

Thank You!

Amen.

❁

What does love look like? It has hands to help others. It has feet to hasten to the poor and needy. It has eyes to see misery and want. It has ears to hear the sighs and sorrows of men. That is what love looks like.

Saint Augustine of Hippo